THE LIFE MANAGEMENT PORTFOLIO

A HOW-TO-GUIDE FOR ORGANIZING YOUR LIFE

ANNI B. JOHNSON

For bulk or special sales, conference, workshop, or vendor opportunities visit:
www.annibjohnson.com

Edition: First

ISBN 978-0-9986580-1-8 (pbk)

Library of Congress Control Number: 2021918831

Interior Design: Aeyshaa
Instagram: aeysha_bookdesign

Cover Design: Ultrakhan22

To my mother who has sacrificed her health and well-being to care for countless family members, neighbors and friends.

To caregivers who tirelessly dedicate themselves to managing the lives of loved ones in need of support.

This workbook belongs to:

_____

_____

CONTENTS

Part I:

YOUR LIFE, FULLY MANAGED

INTRODUCTION

My brother loved riding motorcycles. It had been his passion since he was a kid; and as a carefree young man in his 30s, he often indulged in the amateur racing circuit despite warnings of its risks. My brother was a thrill seeker; a daredevil who lived by the seat of his pants – never worrying about tomorrow when there was excitement to chase today. Until one day, he hit an oil slick on the track that sent him careening into a wall.

It was August 18, 2002. I received a call from the paramedics saying they were air-lifting my brother to a hospital in Charlottesville, Virginia. In that moment, I knew our lives—and his—would never again be the same. My brother was newly married; his son barely a year old. We were in shock as we prepared for the seven-hour drive to Virginia.

My parents, uncle, sister-in-law, nephew, and I arrived at the hospital to learn that my brother had broken his neck in three places and had severe swelling of the brain. The prognosis was grim. He would never walk or care for himself again—that is, if he lived at all. He was unconscious at the time, kept alive by an army of beeping machines. Knowing my brother and how he lived his life, I was the only one who advocated taking him off life support. Everyone else wanted so badly to believe a miracle could save him, even if it meant he could never again choose to live as he'd always lived: to the fullest.

As we sat in the hospital conference room trying to make the heaviest of all decisions, it became painfully clear to us how little information we had. My brother had left no instructions for times like this. No one knew how to contact his workplace, whether his health insurance would cover his hospital bills, or if he had long-term care insurance at all. My brother was fighting for his life, and here we were, powerless to help with even the most mundane matters.

My brother lived for seven years after that in a long-term care facility under 24-hour care, paralyzed from the neck down, before passing away two days shy of his 40th birthday. He lived to see his son go to school and delight in his accomplishments, but he later confessed that he would have opted to be taken off life support rather than spend the rest of his life as a quadriplegic.

I tell you this story to show you that sometimes, awful and unexpected things really do happen in life; but also to help you realize that part of the stress and pain my family experienced could have been avoided. Like so many people, my brother never made a contingency plan for his family, his finances, or his own care, because he never wanted to think that he might need one. But life throws us all curve balls (or oil slicks) sometimes, and it's only by talking about these things, and making a plan before we find ourselves in need of one, that we can be fully and properly prepared.

We all know this, of course—but it's one thing to know you should be prepared and another to actually take the steps to properly prepare your family for a potential crisis. Doing the latter takes accepting that hard decisions will ultimately have to be made, taking initiative to organize all the information someone will need in order to make them, and opening yourself to real conversations with your loved ones to properly inform one another of how to handle certain situations, should they come to pass.

The Life Management Portfolio: A How-To-Guide for Organizing Your Life can help you and your family do all of these things. Not only is it a blueprint for organizing the important information in your life; it also becomes a guidebook for anyone who may have to step into your shoes to care for you, your family, or your personal affairs.

Using your *Life Management Portfolio: A How-To-Guide for Organizing Your Life* is simple. The 13 sections of the workbook, ranging in topics from family and finances to health and advance directives, give you a template to document aspects of your household and your personal and financial information. In the process, you will be prompted to take stock of your policies and accounts, and to update anything that might need your attention—because no life insurance policy is helpful if it cannot be located, the beneficiaries are deceased or no longer in your life!

With every facet of your day-to-day recorded and meticulously organized in this one book, finding information becomes incredibly easy—whether it's yourself looking for policy details, or a friend looking for instructions on how to care for your children in your sudden absence. Having all the information here, in one easy-to-reference book, will give you the peace of mind of knowing that your family will be taken care of with the resources that you've laid out, and in a manner that you've chosen and considered.

The basis of this book comes from my 28 years' experience as a Licensed Social Worker and serving the elderly and disabled communities. I've worked with countless families in the wake of a sudden emergency, witnessed the frantic searches through drawers and cabinets for insurance policies, wills, financial and employment information. Nothing is worse than having to turn over every piece of paper in someone's home, hoping to find some document that may or may not be there at all.

My own parents found themselves in a similar position a few years ago after my father fell and hit his head, causing a brain bleed that required emergency brain surgery. My mother was left scrambling to find answers to a flood of questions, where in the past my father had handled most of their household financial affairs. Could she access their banking information without his credentials? How was she supposed to pay the bills? Every household has that "one person" who takes primary charge of everything, but what if something happens to that one person? Thankfully, my dad was home and recovering within a few weeks, but this was a wake-up call for my parents to make sure both partners were informed and involved in all matters around the house. It was at my parent's urging that I wrote and published this book, to help other families be more proactive about keeping and communicating vital information within a household.

These days, it's especially important to create a reference of the information in our lives simply because there is so much of it, and not all of it is in neat paper files that someone can easily find. With the rise of online banking, smartphones and cloud storage, so much is now kept in digital devices that we rely on our memories to unlock. But what if something should happen to either us or our devices? Your completed *Life Management Portfolio: A How-To-Guide for Organizing Your Life* will serve as a gateway to all this information, should you or someone else need to access it.

As you complete your Portfolio, you will occasionally find that answering these questions is not easy. Yes, some of it is simply a matter of gathering paper records and logging account numbers. While other sections will require you to talk openly with your loved ones about matters such as how each of you want to be commemorated, who will take over guardianship of your minor children, or how to maintain a household or business in your absence. These conversations will be deep, even difficult at times, but I encourage you not to shy away from them any longer. Too many of us only think as we're sitting by a bedside or kneeling before a coffin, *If only we had more time to talk.* So please, talk to your loved ones. Talk to them now. Go through this process together, and know that in doing so; you will have brought your family a level of peace, confidence, and preparedness to handle whatever life may bring.

Chapter **1:**

WHAT WOULD YOU DO?

I magine one day you find yourself in the following situations. I raise these scenarios to be hypothetical, but the reality is that they are not: I myself have lived through some version of these exact moments, and each one led to a cascade of life-changing questions that demanded answers. As you imagine these events (or some version of them) happening to you, ask yourself: *Would you know what to do?*

CASE #1

It's an early Sunday morning and you are awakened by your phone ringing on your nightstand. *Who could be calling this early?* you wonder.

"Hello," you answer sleepily.

"Yes, hi," a male voice says. "This is Police Officer..."

Before you could register the officer's name, you bolt upright in bed.

The officer continues and says that he has an elderly gentleman with him and he found your name and number in his wallet. He reads you the man's name from his license and asks if he's a relative of yours. You're confused. *Why is Dad out and about so early in the morning?* The officer tells you your father was found wandering the grocery store parking lot and a store clerk called 911. He seems confused, but otherwise ok. "Can you come pick him up?" he asks.

"He doesn't have his car?" you ask, slightly alarmed. The grocery store is miles away from your father's home!

The officer thought it was best if someone could come down to get him. In your head, you think, this is likely the start of many things you will have to take care of for your father.

CASE #2

Your 90-year-old grandma lives alone a few states away. You talk to her often on the phone, always asking about her day and her garden. She's always been extremely independent, but you notice she mentions some challenges at home and lately she's been complaining of pain in her legs and back. You finally question her further and decide a visit is necessary to assess things for yourself. After a long day of traveling, you reach her front door and ring the bell. No answer. You knock and peek in through the windows, then call the house phone a few times. Still, no answer. You then remember the old spare key at the back of the shed. You let yourself in the back door and enter to find Grandma on the kitchen floor.

"Grandma! What happened?" you cry out as you rush to her side.

Grandma says in a weak voice, "I came downstairs to make breakfast yesterday and fell, and couldn't get up."

"You've been on the floor since yesterday?!" You begin to cry at the thought of your grandma lying helpless on the floor for over 24 hours alone. Emotions overwhelm you and you start questioning what to do.

CASE #3

You're a 47-year-old single mom working long hours to support your teenage daughter's passion for dance. During the week, you spend most of your time outside of work on pick-ups and drop-offs, and your weekends are full of rehearsals, competitions, fundraising and other activities to support the dance school. You notice a lingering headache that wouldn't go away. You take a few pain killers here and there, and vow to see the doctor as soon as the fall recital is over.

One evening, you suddenly fall ill. With no family members living nearby, your panicked daughter calls one of the dance moms for help. Within hours, you suffer a stroke and are rushed to the emergency room, where you undergo surgery and are then placed on a ventilator. Your daughter sits by your bedside, praying for a miracle.

It's been three weeks, and you still have not regained consciousness. Your aunt arrives from out-of-town and within days, she decides, as your next-of-kin, to remove you from all life-sustaining support. What will happen to your daughter?

CASE #4

Your morning starts off like any other, until you receive a call at work from your wife's phone, except when you pick up it's not your wife speaking. "I'm sorry," a man says, "but there has been an accident. I dialed the last number in her phone. Thank God it was unlocked."

Your heart stops. The caller goes on to describe a woman lying on the ground at the corner of Liberty Avenue and 135th Street, just shy of Lucky Paws Dog Grooming Palace.

You sit there in shock, unable to utter a word. Your wife owns Lucky Paws Dog Grooming Palace and she was going in a bit early today. "Is she ok? Can you put her on the phone?" you ask, almost frantic.

"No," the caller replied. "She seems to be unconscious. Her phone was in her hand. I called 911 immediately, but wanted to see if I could get in touch with anyone from her contacts so they could be aware of what happened."

You can hear the sirens of an approaching ambulance getting louder and louder.

"Can you tell the paramedics who this woman is?" the caller asked.

"Yes," you say, your voice trembling and tears streaming down your face onto the papers outlining your next meeting, scheduled within the hour. "It's my wife."

If it were you driving to pick up your father or helping your grandma off the kitchen floor, leaving your daughter's care to another or stepping in as a temporary manager of Lucky Paws Dog Grooming Palace...Would you know what to do?

Each case presents an uncertain future, and many questions that you and your family will need answers to. Has Dad seen a doctor who can prescribe next steps to manage his early-onset dementia? Does Grandma have long-term care insurance or finances to cover costs if she is no longer able to live alone? Would you have wanted to be taken off life-support, and now that you're gone, who will care for your daughter? If you're like most people, you've probably never openly discussed or thought about these questions before.

No one wants to talk about the scary what-ifs. But would you really trust these life-altering decisions to others—or worse, leave them up to chance? That's exactly what happens when you have no plan in place, so don't wait until you need a plan to make one. By completing your *Life Management Portfolio: A How-To-Guide for Organizing Your Life* today, you will be giving yourself and your family the answers and the confidence to face the future together.

Chapter **2:**
WHO BENEFITS?

Think back to the scenarios from the last chapter for a moment. Now imagine yourself in the aftermath, having to answer all sorts of questions from doctors, lawyers, or financial planners. Now imagine this: Maybe it's not you who gets the phone call. Instead, you're the one going into surgery or riding in the ambulance, and your family is tasked with your care and upholding the household without you for a while. You are not only completing *The Life Management Portfolio: A How-To-Guide for Organizing Your Life* for your own benefit, but so your loved ones can stay informed, knowledgeable and ready! So, what sorts of people can benefit from having this resource, you ask?

Caregivers – Whether you're caring for your parents' affairs or asking a friend to care for your children and pets for a short time, caregivers can use this Portfolio to find answers to everyday questions to keep things running smoothly.

Spouses — It's not uncommon for one partner to be more organized and on top of everything than the other. Use the process of completing your *Life Management Portfolio: A How-To-Guide for Organizing Your Life* as an opportunity to involve and inform both partners and, once it's complete – grab it to seek everyday answers to household questions.

Life partners — Life partners share a big part of their lives together. Be empowered to document everything that's important to know and (legally, if possible) put things in place that offer protections for each other.

Single parents — As head-of-household, a lot rests on your shoulders. Educate your children and close trusted friends or family on how to navigate your home and care for any minor children, should anything ever happen that prevents you from being there for them.

Singles – *The Life Management Portfolio: A How-To-Guide for Organizing Your Life* is just as important for those living alone. Streamlining information in one convenient place makes it that much easier for a trusted friend or family member to step in where needed, and offer assistance in navigating your world, even if temporarily.

Caregivers for persons with disabilities or special needs — A lot can go into caring for an individual with disabilities or special needs, and the continuity of that care can be especially important and difficult to understand without instructions. It's important to fully document the healthcare needs and resources of a loved one with disabilities or special needs, and to have a plan in place in case anyone should have to take over their care.

Physicians — A patient's medical history is crucial for a physician to know when determining appropriate treatment. Help a physician make the most informed decision possible for you and your loved ones by keeping a thorough record of diagnoses, medications, and other must-know medical details in your Portfolio.

Executors — For those tasked to settle the responsibilities of an estate, no matter how big or small, everything will be carefully outlined with no detail left unattended to in this *Life Management Portfolio*.

People facing natural disasters – With the likes of global warming and an increase in volatile weather patterns across the country, *The Life Management Portfolio: A How-To-Guide for Organizing Your Life* provides a wealth of information at your fingertips should your home and its contents suffer unimaginable damage.

Whether you're trying to organize your household, prepare for medical emergencies, or build yourself a backup for any event that could uproot your home life or vital information, let *The Life Management Portfolio: A How-To-Guide for Organizing Your Life* be your guide. Keep it safe and turn to it often.

Chapter **3:**

HOW TO USE YOUR LIFE MANAGEMENT PORTFOLIO:

A How-To-Guide For Organizing Your Life

SOME GENERAL TIPS

Keep *The Life Management Portfolio: A How-To-Guide for Organizing Your Life* **somewhere safe.** It is imperative that you keep your Portfolio safe and secure at all times. Given the sensitive and personal nature of the material, it is highly advisable that you secure your Portfolio with any and all other legal and vital documentation in a waterproof, fire-proof safe within your home. Although your Portfolio can also serve as an invaluable resource tool for everyday occurrences, you must be mindful to always keep it safe by returning it to its secure location once you're done. Your *Life Management Portfolio* must always be treated with the same level of protection you have for your social security number, birth certificate, passwords, and other confidential documents.

File your documents. Each portion of The Life Management Portfolio: *A How-To-Guide for Organizing Your Life* includes a checklist of related documents that are important to complete the information in your Portfolio. It's recommended that you purchase a file organizer to sort and keep these important documents. You may find it helpful to label each file according to the corresponding section of your Portfolio. And, as with the Portfolio itself, it is imperative to keep these documents in a safe, secure location within your home – preferably a locked safe box alongside your *Life Management Portfolio*.

Teach others how to use *The Life Management Portfolio: A How-To-Guide for Organizing Your Life.* Like the information and knowledge kept in *The Life Management Portfolio*, the Portfolio itself is of no use to anyone if it's locked away somewhere no one can access. Familiarize your family members and close trusted friends with the contents and location of your *Life Management Portfolio* so they may use it, should the need arise. Provide instructions on where the Portfolio is kept, and how to open any locks protecting it. But because of the sensitive information *The Life Management Portfolio* contains, be judicious about whom you share its location with, and how.

Don't leave information blank. If you come across a part of the Portfolio that asks for information that applies to you but that you don't know off the top of your head, don't simply skip that section. Do what you know first, and make a note to find the rest of the answers. Talk to your family members, consult your lawyer, unearth old files and sort through everything. It's important that you find the information and organize it now, before you find yourself needing it and either don't know it or have to waste valuable time looking for it. In addition, make sure to seek clarification on any items that you don't fully understand.

Keep the information in *The Life Management Portfolio: A How-To-Guide for Organizing Your Life* up-to-date. You should set aside time once a year to look over everything in your Portfolio to ensure that no changes have been overlooked. This is particularly important if revisions or changes were made to policies, medications, and online passwords, as these tend to change more often than other information. Be sure to sign off on the annual review form at the back of your portfolio to ensure you have conducted an annual assessment.

***

The Life Management Portfolio: **A How-To-Guide for Organizing Your Life workbook is divided into 13 sections:**

1. Family Dynamics
2. Employment Profile
3. Health & Medical Profile
4. Children & Dependents
5. Financial Information
6. Real Estate Profile
7. Household Expenses
8. Vehicle Information
9. Legal Profile
10. Advance Directives
11. Final Wishes
12. Charitable Donations
13. Online Accounts & Login Credentials

At the start of each section, you will find a brief explanation of what each part entails and some helpful tips for organizing your information in that area. At the end of each section, you will find a checklist of important documents you should file alongside *The Life Management Portfolio: A How-to-Guide for Organizing Your Life.*

The information asked for in these sections is meant to be comprehensive, but you will also be given space to note any additional information at various points throughout. Every person, every family, and every household is different, so feel free to assemble your Portfolio in a way that works best for you and your situation. You don't have to complete your Portfolio all at once (but do set a deadline for yourself to avoid procrastination). Take your time, talk to your family members, and let it be a chance for everyone to be involved.

Let's get started!

Part II:

WORKBOOK

1.
FAMILY DYNAMICS

Think of this section like taking attendance. It asks for a general overview of who is living in your home, including you, your spouse or partner, any minor children, and any other persons (or pets) who could be impacted by a life change in your household. It also prompts you to overview some essential details for each family member, including marital and military service records.

 In this section, you will gather information regarding the following areas:

EMERGENCY CONTACTS — Many people nowadays keep emergency contacts listed in their cell phones, but that's likely the least accessible place for anyone else needing to find them. Keeping a clear, up-to-date list here in your Portfolio will guarantee the information is there for anyone needing to call for assistance on your behalf. For senior citizens living alone, it's always a great idea to have emergency contacts posted on the refrigerator.

MARITAL RECORD — Documenting details of your special day may not be as important as the information in most other sections. However, let it serve as a reminder to ensure you have a certified copy of your Marriage Certificate to file with *The Life Management Portfolio: A How-To-Guide for Organizing Your Life*.

MILITARY RECORD — Veterans have a host of health care services available to them through the Veterans Health Administration (VHA). Information about accessing these benefits may be found on a Certificate of Release or Discharge from Active Duty (Form DD214), which all discharged or retired members of the Armed Forces should have among their records. In addition to helping veterans in securing benefits, this form may be used for employment purposes and by funeral directors for arranging funeral services for deceased veterans.

Thank you for your service!

PETS — Let's not forget our furry friends! They are just as much a part of our family as any loved one, but information about their care is rarely shared with others. Pets suffer from anxiety, too. Let's put them and ourselves at ease with a plan, should they ever need to depend on someone other than you for their care.

HELPFUL TIPS

#1 Cell phones now have an emergency and medical ID feature that can be accessed without entering locked passcodes in cases of emergencies.

#2 Minor children without a passport or some other form of government ID can apply for a non-driver's photo identification card at your local Department of Motor Vehicles.

#3 Social Security will never contact you to verify account information or online credentials and passwords.

#4 Visit Social Security Administration online at www.ssa.gov or by calling 1-800-772-1213 for replacement social security cards or with questions about social security retirement, disability and Medicare benefits.

#5 Certified birth and death certificate copies can be obtained by contacting the vital records office in the state in which the birth or death occurred.

#6 Divorce certificate copies may usually be obtained by contacting the Department of Vital Records in the state and/or county in which the divorce took place. Copies of Divorce Decrees may be obtained by contacting the County Clerk's Office in the county of issuance.

FAMILY HOUSEHOLD MEMBERS

List all individuals residing in your primary residence.

HOUSEHOLD MEMBERS	FAMILY MEMBER #1	FAMILY MEMBER #2
Name		
Relationship to #1	(Self)	
Date of Birth		
Social Security #		
Home Phone #		
Cell Phone #		
Cell Unlock Code/Letters/ Patterns		
Business Phone #		
Email Address		
Email Provider		
Email Login		
Email Password		
Business Email		
Business Email Password		
Driver's License #		
State of Issuance		
Passport ID #		
Passport Expiration Date		
Home Address		
City		
State		
Zip Code		

HOUSEHOLD MEMBERS	FAMILY MEMBER #3	FAMILY MEMBER #4
Name		
Relationship to #1		
Date of Birth		
Social Security #		
Home Phone #		
Cell Phone #		
Cell Unlock Code/Letters/ Patterns		
Business Phone #		
Email Address		
Email Provider		
Email Login		
Email Password		
Business Email		
Business Email Password		
Driver's License #		
State of Issuance		
Passport ID #		
Passport Expiration Date		
Home Address		
City		
State		
Zip Code		

HOUSEHOLD MEMBERS	FAMILY MEMBER #5	FAMILY MEMBER #6
Name		
Relationship to #1		
Date of Birth		
Social Security #		
Home Phone #		
Cell Phone #		
Cell Unlock Code/Letters/ Patterns		
Business Phone #		
Email Address		
Email Provider		
Email Login		
Email Password		
Business Email		
Business Email Password		
Driver's License #		
State of Issuance		
Passport ID #		
Passport Expiration Date		
Home Address		
City		
State		
Zip Code		

EMERGENCY CONTACT

Contact #1 should be a close friend or relation and should know about your *Life Management Portfolio: A How-To-Guide for Organizing Your Life*, how to access it and how to use it.

Place this list somewhere easy to access, such as on your refrigerator or in your wallet, especially if you are a senior citizen or have a condition that may require emergency care.

EMERGENCY CONTACTS	CONTACT #1	CONTACT #2
Name		
Home Phone #		
Cell Phone #		
Email Address		
Business Phone #		
Business Email Address		
Home Address		
City		
State		
Zip Code		

EMERGENCY CONTACTS	CONTACT #3	CONTACT #4
Name		
Home Phone #		
Cell Phone #		
Email Address		
Business Phone #		
Business Email Address		
Home Address		
City		
State		
Zip Code		

Additional Information & Updates: (Please be as specific as possible and date all changes.)

_____

_____

_____

_____

_____

_____

_____

_____

_____

_____

1.2 MARITAL RECORD

If you have located an original marriage license, and have included it with your workbook, you may skip this section.

For those interested, feel free to include wedding venue, reception and vendor information below.

MARITAL RECORD	
Spouse/Partner #1 Full Name	
Spouse/Partner #2 Full Name (include Maiden Name)	
Date of Marriage/Union	
Marriage License #	
State of Issuance	
Town	
County	

MARRIAGE CEREMONY	
Name of Venue	
Name of Venue Contact Person	
Office Phone #	
Office Fax #	
Venue Email Address	
Venue Website	
Address of Ceremony	
City	
State	
Zip Code	

OFFICIANT	
Name of Officiant	
Office Phone #	
Officiant Cell Phone #	
Email Address	
Website (if applicable)	

OFFICIANT	
Address	
City	
State	
Zip Code	

WITNESSES	WITNESS #1	WITNESS #2
Name of Witness		
Relationship to Bride or Groom		
Home Phone #		
Cell Phone #		
Email Address		
Address		
City		
State		
Zip Code		

RECEPTION	
Name of Venue	
Name of Venue Contact Person	
Office Phone #	
Office Fax #	
Venue Email Address	
Venue Website	
Address of Reception	
City	
State	
Zip Code	

WEDDING VENDORS & PHONE #	WEDDING VENDORS & PHONE #
1.	6.
2.	7.
3.	8.
4.	9.
5.	10.

1.3 MILITARY RECORD

Locate your original Form DD214, if you haven't already, and review its accuracy. For assistance in obtaining a copy of your Form DD214, go to www.va.gov. *(If you have included your Form DD214 with your Portfolio, you may skip this section.)*

MILITARY RECORD	VETERAN #1
Name	
Date of Birth	
Social Security #	
Home Phone #	
Cell Phone #	
Email Address	
Next of Kin Name and Phone #	
Branch of Service	
Service Number	
Department, Component and Branch or Class	
Grade, Rate or Rank	
Date of Rank	
Pay Grade	
Selective Service Number	
Local Board Number, City, County, State & Zip	
Date Inducted	
Date of Discharge	
Wars Served	
Decorations, Badges, Medals, Honors, etc.	
Current Home Address	
City	
State	
Zip Code	

MILITARY RECORD	VETERAN #2
Name	
Date of Birth	
Social Security #	
Home Phone #	
Cell Phone #	
Email Address	
Next of Kin Name and Phone #	
Branch of Service	
Service Number	
Department, Component and Branch or Class	
Grade, Rate or Rank	
Date of Rank	
Pay Grade	
Selective Service Number	
Local Board Number, City, County, State & Zip	
Date Inducted	
Date of Discharge	
Wars Served	
Decoration, Badges, Medals, Honors, etc.	
Current Home Address	
City	
State	
Zip Code	

VETERANS HEALTH ADMINISTRATION (VHA)

The Department of Veteran Affairs (VA) has also made it easier to access health records, manage appointments, pharmacy services and more, using the VA Patient Portal, My HealtheVet. Visit www.va.gov for more information and account set-up instructions.

VETERANS HEALTH ADMINISTRATION (VHA)	VETERAN # 1
Patient Name	
VA Hospital Name	
VA Hospital Local Phone #	
VA Patient Portal Website	
Patient Portal Login	
Patient Portal Password	
Patient Portal Pin #	
VA Hospital Address	
City	
State	
Zip Code	

VETERANS HEALTH ADMINISTRATION (VHA)	VETERAN # 2
Patient Name	
VA Hospital Name	
VA Hospital Local Phone #	
VA Patient Portal Website	
Patient Portal Login	
Patient Portal Password	
Patient Portal Pin #	
VA Hospital Address	
City	
State	
Zip Code	

VETERANS ADMINISTRATION CLINICS

Indicate what clinic(s) you utilize through the Veterans Health Administration (VHA), along with each clinic's contact number.

CLINICS USED BY VETERAN #1	PATIENT NAME:
1.	6.
2.	7.
3.	8.
4.	9.
5.	10.

CLINICS USED BY VETERAN #2	PATIENT NAME:
1.	6.
2.	7.
3.	8.
4.	9.
5.	10.

Additional Information & Updates: (Please be as specific as possible and date all changes.)

_____
_____
_____
_____
_____
_____
_____
_____
_____
_____
_____
_____

1.4 PETS

Provide information on each of your pets individually. Space is provided to accommodate up to four pets. For any additional pets, be sure to provide the same information in your completed *Life Management Portfolio: A How-To-Guide for Organizing Your Life.*

Pet #1

Name: _____

GENERAL INFORMATION	
Breed	
Sex	M / F
Color	
Date of Birth	
License #	
Registration #	
Microchip Identification #	
Care Instructions *(walk schedule, cleaning schedule, etc.)*	
Brand/Type of Food Used	
Where to Purchase Food	
Feeding Instructions *(quantity, frequency, etc.)*	
Location of Pet Care Items *(leashes, collars, litter, etc.)*	
Behavior Issues	Yes / No *(If yes, explain below)*

VETERINARIAN	ANIMAL HOSPITAL
Doctor's Name	Hospital Name
Doctor's Office Phone #	Hospital Phone #
Emergency Hotline #	Emergency Room #
Email Address	After Hours Emergency #
Veterinarian Website	Email Address
Address	Hospital Website
City	Address
State	City
Zip Code	State & Zip Code

KENNEL		MEDICAL HISTORY	
Kennel Name		Rabies Tag #	
Name of Contact Person		Spayed/Neutered	Yes / No
Office Phone #		Blood Type	
Emergency Hotline #		Existing Conditions	
Email Address		Past Surgeries	
Kennel Website		Current Medications	
Address		Location of Medications	
City		Dosage Instructions *(for multiple medications, list individual instructions below)*	
State		Allergies to Medication	
Zip Code		Allergies to Food	

Additional Information & Updates: (Please be as specific as possible and date all changes.)

_____

_____

_____

_____

_____

_____

_____

_____

_____

_____

_____

Pet #2

Name: _____

GENERAL INFORMATION	
Breed	
Sex	M / F
Color	
Date of Birth	
License #	
Registration #	
Microchip Identification #	
Care Instructions *(walk schedule, cleaning schedule, etc.)*	
Brand/Type of Food Used	
Where to Purchase Food	
Feeding Instructions *(quantity, frequency, etc.)*	
Location of Pet Care Items *(leashes, collars, litter, etc.)*	
Behavior Issues	Yes / No *(If yes, explain below)*

VETERINARIAN		ANIMAL HOSPITAL	
Doctor's Name		Hospital Name	
Doctor's Office Phone #		Hospital Phone #	
Emergency Hotline #		Emergency Room #	
Email Address		After Hours Emergency #	
Veterinarian Website		Email Address	
Address		Hospital Website	
City		Address	
State		City	
Zip Code		State & Zip Code	

KENNEL		MEDICAL HISTORY	
Kennel Name		Rabies Tag #	
Name of Contact Person		Spayed/Neutered	Yes / No
Office Phone #		Blood Type	
Emergency Hotline #		Existing Conditions	
Email Address		Past Surgeries	
Kennel Website		Current Medications	
Address		Location of Medications	
City		Dosage Instructions (*for multiple medications, list individual instructions below*)	
State		Allergies to Medication	
Zip Code		Allergies to Food	

Additional Information & Updates: (Please be as specific as possible and date all changes.)

_____

_____

_____

_____

_____

_____

_____

_____

_____

_____

_____

_____

Pet #3

Name: _____

GENERAL INFORMATION	
Breed	
Sex	M / F
Color	
Date of Birth	
License #	
Registration #	
Microchip Identification #	
Brand/Type of Food Used	
Care Instructions (walk schedule, cleaning schedule, etc.)	
Where to Purchase Food	
Feeding Instructions (quantity, frequency, etc.)	
Location of Pet Care Items (leashes, collars, litter, etc.)	
Behavior Issues	Yes / No (If yes, explain below)

VETERINARIAN	ANIMAL HOSPITAL
Doctor's Name	Hospital Name
Doctor's Office Phone #	Hospital Phone #
Emergency Hotline #	Emergency Room #
Email Address	After Hours Emergency #
Veterinarian Website	Email Address
Address	Hospital Website
City	Address
State	City
Zip Code	State & Zip Code

KENNEL	MEDICAL HISTORY	
Kennel Name	Rabies Tag #	
Name of Contact Person	Spayed/Neutered	Yes / No
Office Phone #	Blood Type	
Emergency Hotline #	Existing Conditions	
Email Address	Past Surgeries	
Kennel Website	Current Medications	
Address	Location of Medications	
City	Dosage Instructions (for multiple medications, list individual instructions below)	
State	Allergies to Medication	
Zip Code	Allergies to Food	

Additional Information & Updates: (Please be as specific as possible and date all changes.)

_____
_____
_____
_____
_____
_____
_____
_____
_____
_____
_____
_____

Pet #4

Name: _____

GENERAL INFORMATION	
Breed	
Sex	M / F
Color	
Date of Birth	
License #	
Registration #	
Microchip Identification #	
Care Instructions *(walk schedule, cleaning schedule, etc.)*	
Brand/Type of Food Used	
Where to Purchase Food	
Feeding Instructions *(quantity, frequency, etc.)*	
Location of Pet Care Items *(leashes, collars, litter, etc.)*	
Behavior Issues	Yes / No *(If yes, explain below)*

VETERINARIAN	ANIMAL HOSPITAL
Doctor's Name	Hospital Name
Doctor's Office Phone #	Hospital Phone #
Emergency Hotline #	Emergency Room #
Email Address	After Hours Emergency #
Veterinarian Website	Email Address
Address	Hospital Website
City	Address
State	City
Zip Code	State & Zip Code

KENNEL		MEDICAL HISTORY	
Kennel Name		Rabies Tag #	
Name of Contact Person		Spayed/Neutered	Yes / No
Office Phone #		Blood Type	
Emergency Hotline #		Existing Conditions	
Email Address		Past Surgeries	
Kennel Website		Current Medications	
Address		Location of Medications	
City		Dosage Instructions *(for multiple medications, list individual instructions below)*	
State		Allergies to Medication	
Zip Code		Allergies to Food	

Additional Information & Updates: (Please be as specific as possible and date all changes.)

_____

_____

_____

_____

_____

_____

_____

_____

_____

_____

_____

FAMILY DYNAMICS DOCUMENT CHECKLIST

Include copies or originals of the following documents with your *Life Management Portfolio: A How-To-Guide for Organizing Your Life*. Make sure to include these documents for each family member residing within your household (*if applicable*), especially for minor children.

The Basics:

☐ Driver's license/government issued photo identification

☐ Passports

☐ Birth certificates

☐ Death certificates

☐ Divorce certificates/divorce decrees

☐ Social security cards

☐ Marriage license

☐ Children's photo identification cards with fingerprints *(if applicable)*

☐ Individual photos of each family member – full-face and full-body images

☐ Church affiliations membership letter

For Veterans:

☐ Form DD214

Pet Records:

☐ Full-face and full-body photos of pets

☐ Veterinarian pet cards

☐ Pet's vaccination records

☐ Pet's microchip card *(if applicable)*

☐ Surgery records

☐ Pet insurance card (front and back)

☐ Pet insurance policy documents

Notes - Explanation for items left unchecked:

_____
_____
_____
_____
_____
_____
_____
_____
_____

2.
EMPLOYMENT PROFILE

Surveys show that more than 50% of Americans change jobs every one to five years. Additionally, over a quarter of Americans were considered self-employed at some point in 2019. Coupled with the fact that your employment status determines so many important details of your life, from health coverage and your paycheck to disability and life insurance, keeping your latest employment information on hand is crucial. It can be the first road sign to someone looking to help you activate certain employment benefits, or an indication to that person that you may be independently insured as a self-employed business owner. For the latter, this section is also vitally important for ensuring that the business you've worked so hard to build can be sustained in your absence.

➢ *In this section, you will gather information regarding the following areas:*

CURRENT EMPLOYMENT INFORMATION – Many of life's important details, from your health benefits to sick leave policies to when you are paid and into what account, all depend on your employer, so it's important that this information is kept current and well-documented. This will be especially useful for anyone needing to access your benefits information on your behalf, or needing funds to continue running your household.

SELF-EMPLOYMENT — If you're an entrepreneur who has worked hard to build a successful business or starting one, you're probably very used to sharing your vision and goals—but how often do you share the actual details of running your business or the management structures that keep it standing? This section gives an overall snapshot of your business and overviews the "paperwork" side of things. While this outline cannot cover the innermost workings of your business, it will help someone running it in your absence to sustain it in the short-term.

HELPFUL TIPS

#1 Review employee benefits yearly and address any discrepancies.

#2 Make updates to your address, emergency contact information, or beneficiaries to employee related programs or policies.

#3 If you have not signed up for a benefit that you are eligible for, contact your Benefits Administrator to discuss your options.

#4 Document multiple direct deposits. That includes social security, Veterans Administration (VA), disability checks, and/or retirement.

#5 Business owners should always keep their files up-to-date so they reflect current business operations.

2.1 EMPLOYMENT

CURRENT EMPLOYMENT

If you are retired or unemployed, you may provide information regarding your last employer or opt to skip this section. Keep in mind, however, of the importance of documenting funds received while retired.

CURRENT EMPLOYMENT	FAMILY MEMBER #1	FAMILY MEMBER #2
Employee Name		
Employer/Company Name		
Date of Hire		
Date of Separation		
Job Title		
Human Resources Phone #	Ext.	Ext.
Human Resources Fax #		
Employee Business Email Address		
Employee Business Email Password		
Main/Switchboard #		
Director/Supervisor Name		
Director/Supervisor Phone #	Ext.	Ext.
Director/Supervisor Cell #		
Director/Supervisor Fax #		
Director/Supervisor Email		
Employer Address		
City		
State		
Zip Code		

EMPLOYEE BENEFITS PACKAGE(S)

EMPLOYEE BENEFITS PACKAGE(S)	FAMILY MEMBER #1	FAMILY MEMBER #2
Employee Name		
Time Accrued (*Circle one*)	Wkly / Bi-Wkly / Mthly / Yearly	Wkly / Bi-Wkly / Mthly / Yearly
Amount of Vacation Days per Year		
Amount of Sick Days per Year		
Amount of Personal Days per Year		
Amount of Holidays per Year		
Amount of Family Leave Days per Year		
Health Insurance (*Circle One*)	Yes / No	Yes / No
Dental Insurance (*Circle One*)	Yes / No	Yes / No
Vision Insurance (*Circle One*)	Yes / No	Yes / No
Prescription Drug Coverage (*Circle One*)	Yes / No	Yes / No
Mental Health Insurance (*Circle One*)	Yes / No	Yes / No

EMPLOYEE BENEFITS ADMINISTRATOR

The Benefits Administrator oversees and handles the contractual side of employee benefit programs such as health care, long and short-term disability insurance, company sponsored life insurance, worker's compensation, pensions and specialty services. In emergencies, the Benefits Administrator serves as a liaison between you and your benefit providers to help you navigate your benefits packages.

EMPLOYEE BENEFITS ADMINISTRATOR	FAMILY MEMBER #1	FAMILY MEMBER #2
Family Member Name		
Benefits Administrator Name		
Person of Contact Name		
Office Phone #	Ext.	Ext.
Office Fax #		
Email Address		
Benefit Administrator Website		
Benefits Employee Portal Login		
Benefits Employee Portal Password		
Benefits Employee Pin #		

Benefits Administrator Address		
City		
State		
Zip Code		

UNION MEMBER BENEFITS

UNION MEMBER BENEFITS	FAMILY MEMBER #1	FAMILY MEMBER #2
Family Member Name		
Union Affiliation		
Union President Name		
Union Person of Contact Name	Ext.	Ext.
Union Office Phone #		
Union Office Fax #		
Union Email Address		
Union Website		
Union Employee Portal Login		
Union Employee Portal Password		
Union Employee Pin #		
Union Address		
City		
State		
Zip Code		

EMPLOYEE PAYROLL

EMPLOYEE PAYROLL	FAMILY MEMBER #1	FAMILY MEMBER #2
Family Member Name		
Pay Period	Wkly / Bi-Wkly / Mthly / Yearly	Wkly / Bi-Wkly / Mthly / Yearly
Pay Day (Circle One)	M / Tu / W / Th / Fr / Sa / Su	M / Tu / W / Th / Fr / Sa / Su
Garnishment(s) (Circle One)	Child Support / Alimony / Other	Child Support / Alimony / Other
Garnishment: Other (Explain)		
Payroll Department Contact		
Payroll Office #		
Payroll Fax #		
Payroll Email Address		
Payroll Website (if applicable)		
Payroll Employee Portal Login		

Payroll Employee Portal Password		
Payroll Employee Pin #		
Payroll Address		
City		
State		
Zip Code		

DIRECT DEPOSIT ACCOUNT

Do not ignore this section if you are retired or a veteran. If you receive direct deposits from the Social Security Administration (SSA) or Veteran Administration (VA), this section applies to you.

DIRECT DEPOSIT ACCOUNT	FAMILY MEMBER #1	FAMILY MEMBER #2
Family Member Name		
Bank Name		
Account Holder Name		
Joint Account (Circle One)	Yes / No	Yes / No
Joint Account Member Name		
Amount Direct Deposited	$	$
Frequency	Wkly / Bi-Wkly / Mthly / Yearly	Wkly / Bi-Wkly / Mthly / Yearly
Account Type (Circle One)	Savings / Checking	Savings / Checking
Type of Deposit (Circle One)	Payroll / SSA / Pension / VA / Other	Payroll / SSA / Pension / VA / Other
Account #		
Routing #		
Local Bank Main Phone #		
Bank Fax #		
Bank Website		
Bank Login		
Bank Password		
Bank Pin #		
Security Word/Code		
Security Questions & Answers		
2-Step Verification Enabled	Yes / No	Yes / No
2-Step Verification (Circle One)	Email / Cell Phone #	Email / Cell Phone #
2-Step Verification Email		
2-Step Verification Email Password		
2-Step Verification Cell Phone #		
Banking Address		

City		
State		
Zip Code		

If you use multiple banks for multiple direct deposits, please indicate that information below.

Additional Information & Updates: (Please be as specific as possible and date all changes.)

_____

_____

_____

_____

_____

_____

_____

_____

_____

2.2 SELF-EMPLOYMENT

Self-Owned Company #1

COMPANY INFORMATION

Family Member Name	
Title/Position Held	
Professional License #	
Company Name	
Company Office Phone #	
Company Fax #	
Company Email Address	
Company Email Provider	
Company Email Login	
Company Email Password	
Company Website	
Company Business Address	
City	
State	
Zip Code	
Company Mailing Address	
City	
State	
Zip Code	

PROFESSIONAL LIABILITY INSURANCE

Liability Insurance Company	
Policy #	
Effective Date of Policy	
Expiration Date of Policy	
Agent Office Phone #	
Agent Cell Phone #	
Agent Email Address	
Company Website	
Client Portal Login	
Client Portal Password	
Client Portal Pin #	

Insurance Company Address	
City	
State	
Zip Code	

BUSINESS STRUCTURE

Type of Business/Industry	
Entity Type (LLC, S-Corp, etc.)	
State of Issuance	
Date of Secretary of State Certificate	
Employer Identification # (EIN)	
Tax Identification # (TIN)	
National Provider Identifier-NPI	
Professional License #/State of Issuance	
Registered Agent Name	
Agent Phone #	
Agent Address	
City	
State	
Zip Code	

BUSINESS LEADERSHIP

President Name	
President Cell Phone #	
President Email Address	
Vice President Name	
VP Cell Phone #	
VP Email Address	
Chief Executive Officer (CEO)	
CEO Cell Phone #	
CEO Email Address	
Chief Financial Officer (CFO)	
CFO Cell Phone #	
CFO Email Address	
Chief Operating Officer (COO)	
COO Cell Phone #	
COO Email Address	
Business Attorney	

Attorney Cell Phone #	
Attorney Email Address	
Professional Executor	
Executor Cell Phone #	
Executor Email Address	

BUSINESS ACCOUNTANT/TAX ACCOUNTANT

Business Accountant Name	
Accountant Company Name	
Accountant Office Phone #	
Accountant Cell Phone #	
Accountant Email Address	
Accountant Website	
Accountant Client Portal Login	
Accountant Client Portal Password	
Accountant Client Portal Pin #	
Accountant Address	
City	
State	
Zip Code	
Tax Accountant (*If Different*)	
Tax Accountant Name	
Tax Accountant Company Name	
Tax Accountant Office Phone #	
Tax Accountant Cell Phone #	
Tax Accountant Email Address	
Tax Accountant Website	
Tax Accountant Client Portal Login	
Tax Accountant Client Portal Password	
Tax Accountant Client Portal Pin #	
Tax Accountant Address	
City	
State	
Zip Code	

BUSINESS BANKING

Bank Name	
Account Holder Name	
Joint Account (*Circle one*)	Yes / No
Joint Account Member Name	
Account Type	Savings
Account #	
Routing #	
Account Type	Checking
Account #	
Routing #	
Toll-Free Banking Phone #	
Local Branch Person of Contact	
Local Branch Phone #	Ext.
Local Branch Fax #	
Point of Contact Email Address	
Business Banking Website	
Business Banking Login	
Business Banking Password	
Business Banking Pin #	
Security Word/Code	
Security Question & Answers	
2-Step Verification Enabled	Yes / No
2-Step Verification (*Circle one*)	Email / Cell Phone #
2-Step Verification Email	
2-Step Verification Email Password	
2-Step Verification Cell Phone #	
Local Branch Address	
City	
State	
Zip Code	

MERCHANT ACCOUNT SERVICES

Merchant Name	
Merchant Phone #	
Account Holder Name	
Joint Account (*Circle one*)	Yes / No

Joint Account Member Name	
Business Account Name	
Account #	
Security Word/Code	
Merchant Website	
Merchant User Login	
Merchant User Password	
Merchant User Pin #	
2-Step Verification Enabled	Yes / No
2-Step Verification (*Circle one*)	Email / Cell Phone #
2-Step Verification Email	
2-Step Verification Email Password	
2-Step Verification Cell Phone #	

BUSINESS WEBSITE

Website Platform Used	
Website Domain Name	
Company Domain Name Registered With	
Website Login	
Website Password	
Website Pin #	
Website Expiration Date	
Website Design Company	
Website Designer Name	
Designer Website	
Designer Office Phone #	
Designer Cell Phone #	
Designer Maintenance Package	Yes / No
Website Designer Address	
City	
State	
Zip Code	
Website Content Creator Name	
Content Creator Website	
Content Creator Office Phone #	
Content Creator Cell Phone #	
Content Maintenance Package	Yes / No

BUSINESS SOCIAL MEDIA ACCOUNTS

Business Facebook Page Name	
Personal Facebook Page Name	
Facebook Login	
Facebook Password	
Facebook Administrator Name	
Facebook Admin Phone #	
Facebook Admin Cell Phone #	
Business Instagram Page Name	
Instagram Login	
Instagram Password	
Instagram Administrator Name	
Instagram Admin Office Phone #	
Instagram Admin Cell Phone #	
Business Twitter Page Name	
Twitter Login	
Twitter Password	
Twitter Administrator Name	
Twitter Admin Office Phone #	
Twitter Admin Cell Phone #	
Business LinkedIn Page Name	
LinkedIn Login	
LinkedIn Password	
LinkedIn Administrator Name	
LinkedIn Admin Office Phone #	
LinkedIn Admin Cell Phone #	
Clubhouse User Name	
Clubhouse @name	
Clubhouse Cell Phone #	

BUSINESS VENDORS

BUSINESS VENDORS & PHONE #	BUSINESS VENDORS & PHONE #
1.	1.
2.	2.
3.	3.
4.	4.
5.	5.
6.	6.
7.	7.

BUSINESS INVESTORS

BUSINESS INVESTORS NAMES & CELL PHONE #	BUSINESS INVESTORS NAMES & CELL PHONE #
1.	1.
2.	2.
3.	3.
4.	4.
5.	5.
6.	6.
7.	7.

Additional Information & Updates: (Please be as specific as possible and date all changes.)

_____

_____

_____

_____

_____

_____

Self-Owned Company #2

COMPANY INFORMATION

Family Member Name	
Title/Position Held	
Professional License #	
Company Name	
Company Office Phone #	
Company Fax #	
Company Email Address	
Company Email Provider	
Company Email Login	
Company Email Password	
Company Website	
Company Business Address	
City	
State	
Zip Code	

Company Mailing Address	
City	
State	
Zip Code	

PROFESSIONAL LIABILITY INSURANCE

Liability Insurance Company	
Policy #	
Effective Date of Policy	
Expiration Date of Policy	
Agent Office Phone #	
Agent Cell Phone #	
Agent Email Address	
Company Website	
Client Portal Login	
Client Portal Password	
Client Portal Pin #	
Insurance Company Address	
City	
State	
Zip Code	

BUSINESS STRUCTURE

Type of Business/Industry	
Entity Type (LLC, S-Corp, etc.)	
State of Issuance	
Date of Secretary of State Certificate	
Employer Identification # (EIN)	
Tax Identification # (TIN)	
National Provider Identifier-NPI	
Professional License #/State of Issuance	
Registered Agent Name	
Agent Phone #	
Agent Address	
City	
State	
Zip Code	

BUSINESS LEADERSHIP

President Name	
President Cell Phone #	
President Email Address	
Vice President Name	
VP Cell Phone #	
VP Email Address	
Chief Executive Officer (CEO)	
CEO Cell Phone #	
CEO Email Address	
Chief Financial Officer (CFO)	
CFO Cell Phone #	
CFO Email Address	
Chief Operating Officer (COO)	
COO Cell Phone #	
COO Email Address	
Business Attorney	
Attorney Cell Phone #	
Attorney Email Address	
Professional Executor	
Executor Cell Phone #	
Executor Email Address	

BUSINESS ACCOUNTANT/TAX ACCOUNTANT

Business Accountant Name	
Accountant Company Name	
Accountant Office Phone #	
Accountant Cell Phone #	
Accountant Email Address	
Accountant Website	
Accountant Client Portal Login	
Accountant Client Portal Password	
Accountant Client Portal Pin #	
Accountant Address	
City	
State	
Zip Code	
Tax Accountant (*If Different*)	

Tax Accountant Name	
Tax Accountant Company Name	
Tax Accountant Office Phone #	
Tax Accountant Cell Phone #	
Tax Accountant Email Address	
Tax Accountant Website	
Tax Accountant Client Portal Login	
Tax Accountant Client Portal Password	
Tax Accountant Client Portal Pin #	
Tax Accountant Address	
City	
State	
Zip Code	

BUSINESS BANKING

Bank Name	
Account Holder Name	
Joint Account (*Circle one*)	Yes / No
Joint Account Member Name	
Account Type	Savings
Account #	
Routing #	
Account Type	Checking
Account #	
Routing #	
Toll-Free Banking Phone #	
Local Branch Person of Contact	
Local Branch Phone #	Ext.
Local Branch Fax #	
Point of Contact Email Address	
Business Banking Website	
Business Banking Login	
Business Banking Password	
Business Banking Pin #	
Security Word/Code	
Security Question & Answers	
2-Step Verification Enabled	Yes / No

2-Step Verification (*Circle one*)	Email / Cell Phone #
2-Step Verification Email	
2-Step Verification Email Password	
2-Step Verification Cell Phone #	
Local Branch Address	
City	
State	
Zip Code	

MERCHANT ACCOUNT SERVICES

Merchant Name	
Merchant Phone #	
Account Holder Name	
Joint Account (*Circle one*)	Yes / No
Joint Account Member Name	
Business Account Name	
Account #	
Security Word/Code	
Merchant Website	
Merchant User Login	
Merchant User Password	
Merchant User Pin #	
2-Step Verification Enabled	Yes / No
2-Step Verification (*Circle one*)	Email / Cell Phone #
2-Step Verification Email	
2-Step Verification Email Password	
2-Step Verification Cell Phone #	

BUSINESS WEBSITE

Website Platform Used	
Website Domain Name	
Company Domain Name Registered With	
Website Login	
Website Password	
Website Pin #	
Website Expiration Date	
Website Design Company	
Website Designer Name	

Designer Website	
Designer Office Phone #	
Designer Cell Phone #	
Designer Maintenance Package	Yes / No
Website Designer Address	
City	
State	
Zip Code	
Website Content Creator Name	
Content Creator Website	
Content Creator Office Phone #	
Content Creator Cell Phone #	
Content Maintenance Package	Yes / No

BUSINESS SOCIAL MEDIA ACCOUNTS

Business Facebook Page Name	
Personal Facebook Page Name	
Facebook Login	
Facebook Password	
Facebook Administrator Name	
Facebook Admin Phone #	
Facebook Admin Cell Phone #	
Business Instagram Page Name	
Instagram Login	
Instagram Password	
Instagram Administrator Name	
Instagram Admin Office Phone #	
Instagram Admin Cell Phone #	
Business Twitter Page Name	
Twitter Login	
Twitter Password	
Twitter Administrator Name	
Twitter Admin Office Phone #	
Twitter Admin Cell Phone #	
Business LinkedIn Page Name	
LinkedIn Login	
LinkedIn Password	
LinkedIn Administrator Name	
LinkedIn Admin Office Phone #	

LinkedIn Admin Cell Phone #	
Clubhouse User Name	
Clubhouse @name	
Clubhouse Cell Phone #	

BUSINESS VENDORS

BUSINESS VENDORS & PHONE #	BUSINESS VENDORS & PHONE #
1.	1.
2.	2.
3.	3.
4.	4.
5.	5.
6.	6.
7.	7.

BUSINESS INVESTORS

BUSINESS INVESTORS NAMES & CELL PHONE #	BUSINESS INVESTORS NAMES & CELL PHONE #
1.	1.
2.	2.
3.	3.
4.	4.
5.	5.
6.	6.
7.	7.

Additional Information & Updates: (Please be as specific as possible and date all changes.)

_____

_____ _____

_____ _____

_____ _____

_____ _____

_____ _____

EMPLOYMENT PROFILE DOCUMENT CHECKLIST

Include a copy or originals of the following documents with your *Life Management Portfolio: A How-To-Guide for Organizing Your Life.*

Employment:

☐ Employee Identification Card (front and back)

☐ Employment Offer Letter and Employment Contract *(if applicable)*

☐ Direct Deposit Pay Stub

☐ Bank statements where each direct deposit is made *(if applicable)*

☐ Union Identification Card (front and back)

☐ Union Benefits Contract

Self-Employment or Self-Owned Company:

☐ Secretary of State Business Entity Certificate (LLC, S-Corp, etc.)

☐ Business Credit Card statement

☐ Business Debit Card statement

☐ Employee Identification Number (EIN)

☐ Tax Identification Number (TIN)

☐ Professional Liability Insurance Certificate

☐ Professional License *(if applicable)*

☐ Business Contracts

☐ Tax Returns (past seven years)

☐ Business Banking Statements

Notes - Explanation for items left unchecked:

_____

_____

_____

_____

_____

_____

_____

3.
HEALTH & MEDICAL PROFILE

Out of all the sections of this workbook, this is one of the most essential. Medical decisions are probably some the hardest we ever have to make: they often have to be made quickly, carry life-or-death consequences, require full knowledge of a patient's health history, and call for you to consider a complex matrix of insurance information. Not to mention, emotions are probably running high and everyone is stressed, especially if you're dealing with an unexpected health crisis.

But if you can handle at least some of those factors ahead of time by completing your *Life Management Portfolio: A How-To-Guide for Organizing Your Life,* you give yourself a better chance of making well-informed decisions and experiencing less stress in the moment. You will also be helping others to make the best decisions possible, whether they are physicians, hospital administrators, or your own family members.

While the information in this section will certainly help anyone dealing with an unexpected health crisis, having this information readily on-hand is helpful as well for handling routine care, and especially for the elderly. Greater need for all sorts of medical care is likely to arise as you, your parents, or your grandparents reach the golden years, making it all the more important that you understand the benefits and resources available to you and your family. Having all the information organized and having a strong support system in place will allow you to meet any health challenges or medical decisions head on.

NOTE: This section is meant to cover only the two heads of household: Family Member #1 and a partner/spouse, Family Member #2. (Health and medical information about minor children are covered in the next section, Children & Dependents.)

 In this section, you will gather information regarding the following areas:

GENERAL HEALTH OVERVIEW — Continuity of care is best supported when everyone is involved. This section will help you document your medical history, medications, diagnoses, surgeries and more, all in one place. Having the full picture is essential when you're faced with having to make life-altering decisions.

HEALTH INSURANCE & PRESCRIPTION COVERAGE — This is a challenging section because it asks for a comprehensive overview of all the benefits and services offered under your health plan(s). You'll explore copayment, deductibles, in-network and out-of-network policies, just to name a few. As complicated as insurance plans may be, take the time to really understand your health coverage.

MEDICARE is for senior citizens aged 65 and older. Often referred to as "the red, white and blue card," there are four parts to Medicare coverage – Parts A, B, C and D. Each part covers different areas of medical need.

Part A – Covers hospital expenses such as room, board and various inpatient services. It also covers ambulance services, limited stay in a skilled nursing facility, hospice care, and intermittent home health care.

Part B – Covers doctor services, outpatient care, some preventative services, and durable medical equipment (DME) costs. It also covers some occupational and physical services, and some home health care.

Part C – An all-in-one plan known as Medicare Advantage, Part C is inclusive of benefits in Parts A and B, and may also include Medicare Part D (prescription drug coverage).

Part D – Also called the Medicare prescription drug benefit, is an optional program to help cover prescription costs.

Medicare pays 80% of your medical expenses. The remaining 20% is the policy holder's responsibility, unless you have enrolled in supplemental insurance to cover the remaining balance.

MEDICAID is a federal and state health insurance program that covers medical expenses for those who qualify based on their level of income. However, Medicaid often enters the picture also for elderly patients if they require long-term care. One of the differences between Medicare and Medicaid is that while Medicare will typically cover post-hospital care for up to six weeks after hospitalization, it does not cover long-term home care services, while Medicaid does. Medicaid covers services such as skilled nursing home care and personal care at home, as well as some community-based services like Adult Day Health Care Services. For this reason, Medicaid planning usually becomes a priority when an elderly parent or grandparent needs to explore long-term care options.

PHYSICIANS & SERVICES — Whether you only visit your doctor for routine preventative care or you have a chronic condition that requires ongoing monitoring by a specialist, we all choose our doctors carefully and like to know that our care is being overseen by physicians we have grown to know, and who know our medical histories. Documenting your medical team in your Portfolio will help ensure continuity of care, decrease confusion, and provide you the comfort of knowing you will be seen by a professional of your choosing (in most cases).

DENTAL COVERAGE & SERVICES — Dental coverage is often separate from regular health insurance. Filling out this section is important for providing a complete picture of your dental care.

VISION COVERAGE & SERVICES — As with dental coverage, vision benefits are often separate from your typical health plan and should therefore be documented here. In addition, vision care can include much more than an annual eye exam to see if you need glasses for reading or driving, and can involve a number of different professionals. Optometrists assess the general health of your eyes, and handle vision changes pertaining to testing, correction and management. Opticians are trained technicians who specialize in the fit of eyeglasses and contact lenses. Ophthalmologists, on the other hand, are medical doctors specializing in diagnosing and treating diseases of the eye, as well as performing eye surgeries and monitoring the overall health of the eyes.

SPECIALTY MEDICAL COVERAGE & SERVICES — Some employers offer various policies, such as short-term disability and life insurance policies, or specialty medical coverage for specific health challenges such as infertility. Take the opportunity to explore what specialty benefits are available to you by contacting your insurance company or your Employee Benefits Administrator. For any benefits you have already enrolled in, you want to make sure you are up-to-date on premiums and that your policy is still active. Nothing is worse than thinking you have a policy in place when you actually do not!

MENTAL HEALTH COVERAGE & SERVICES — Mental health care can be one of the most difficult forms of health care to access, in part due to the stigma associated with needing help. But for those needing support in this area, continuity of care and the relief of knowing what's covered and what's not, are especially crucial to ensuring health and well-being.

HELPFUL TIPS

#1 Health alerts can be life threatening. Whether it's a medication or food allergy, or preference for organ donation, talk to your family so they are aware, and can be better advocates when needed.

#2 Medicare pays only 80% of medical expenses - but you could supplement the remaining 20% of expenses with supplemental insurance. Visit www.medicare.gov for more information.

#3 Electronic Medical Records (EMR) allow you to access your health records and information on the go. Check with your medical provider for details.

#4 Communicate with your doctors. Let them know what other specialist you are seeing and for what reason.

#5 If you participate in Mail Ordered Prescriptions, make sure you fully complete information pertaining to this in your *Life Management Portfolio: A How-To-Guide for Organizing Your Life*.

#6 Copayments and deductibles vary year to year, so keep a log of when they change.

#7 You can request copies of radiology and lab reports from your doctor(s) for your files.

#8 Routine ophthalmology care should be a part of your annual health exam schedule.

#9 Medical Storage pertains to embryos, umbilical cord, ovum, and semen. It's imperative that you carefully document this information, should anyone need to inquire on your behalf.

#10 Explore long-term Care options and benefits sooner rather than later. There is a lot of free information out there regarding Medicaid, Medicare, Skilled Nursing, Home Care, and Companion Care, to name a few. It's best to educate yourself on these services before the need arises.

#11 Any information that could offer you comfort in time of need should be specifically stated, including any special laboratory circumstances. For example, if blood can only be drawn from the left arm, you have small veins, or you have a port, that information should be highlighted in your workbook.

#12 Do not be ashamed to record all the pieces of your medical picture; it will simply be to provide you the best care possible, and that requires a full and honest history of your health, including possible illnesses that may be hard to discuss.

#13 Health Insurance Portability and Accountability Act (HIPAA) is a federal law that protects patient health information from being disclosed without the patient's consent or knowledge. For more information on how to authorize consent, visit www.hhs.gov.

3.1 GENERAL HEALTH OVERVIEW

Family Member #1

Name: _____

HEALTH ALERTS

Health Alerts	
Date of Birth	
Blood Type	
Medication Allergies	
Food Allergies	

Additional Information & Updates: (Please be as specific as possible and date all changes.)

_____

_____

_____

_____

_____

_____

_____

_____

_____

_____

_____

DIAGNOSES

Diagnosis		Diagnosis	
Year Diagnosed		Year Diagnosed	
Doctor		Doctor	
Surgery	Yes / No	Surgery	Yes / No
If yes, Date of Surgery		If yes, Date of Surgery	
Final Report Attached	Yes / No	Final Report Attached	Yes / No

Diagnosis		Diagnosis	
Year Diagnosed		Year Diagnosed	
Doctor		Doctor	
Surgery	Yes / No	Surgery	Yes / No
If yes, Date of Surgery		If yes, Date of Surgery	
Final Report Attached	Yes / No	Final Report Attached	Yes / No

Diagnosis		Diagnosis	
Year Diagnosed		Year Diagnosed	
Doctor		Doctor	
Surgery	Yes / No	Surgery	Yes / No
If yes, Date of Surgery		If yes, Date of Surgery	
Final Report Attached	Yes / No	Final Report Attached	Yes / No

Additional Information & Updates: (Please be as specific as possible and date all changes.)

_____

_____

_____

_____

_____

_____

_____

_____

_____

_____

MEDICATIONS

Medication Name	Medication Name
Dosage	Dosage
Route (by mouth, injected, etc.)	Route (by mouth, injected, etc.)
Frequency (how often taken)	Frequency (how often taken)
Indication (reason for taking)	Indication (reason for taking)
Prescribing Doctor	Prescribing Doctor

Medication Name	Medication Name
Dosage	Dosage
Route (by mouth, injected, etc.)	Route (by mouth, injected, etc.)
Frequency (how often taken)	Frequency (how often taken)

Indication (*reason for taking*)	Indication (*reason for taking*)
Prescribing Doctor	Prescribing Doctor

Medication Name	**Medication Name**
Dosage	Dosage
Route (*by mouth, injected, etc.*)	Route (*by mouth, injected, etc.*)
Frequency (*how often taken*)	Frequency (*how often taken*)
Indication (*reason for taking*)	Indication (*reason for taking*)
Prescribing Doctor	Prescribing Doctor

Medication Name	**Medication Name**
Dosage	Dosage
Route (*by mouth, injected, etc.*)	Route (*by mouth, injected, etc.*)
Frequency (*how often taken*)	Frequency (*how often taken*)
Indication (*reason for taking*)	Indication (*reason for taking*)
Prescribing Doctor	Prescribing Doctor

Medication Name	**Medication Name**
Dosage	Dosage
Route (*by mouth, injected, etc.*)	Route (*by mouth, injected, etc.*)
Frequency (*how often taken*)	Frequency (*how often taken*)
Indication (*reason for taking*)	Indication (*reason for taking*)
Prescribing Doctor	Prescribing Doctor

Additional Information & Updates: (Please be as specific as possible and date all changes.)

_____

_____

_____

_____

_____

_____

_____

_____

_____

_____

If you have received **Durable Medical Equipment (DME)** supplies or any assistive devices, be sure to itemize them below. *(Wheelchairs, hospital beds, walkers, oxygen, hearing aids, etc.)*

ASSISTIVE DEVICE	PRESCRIBING DOCTOR	DME SUPPLY COMPANY	PHONE #

Additional Information & Updates: (Please be as specific as possible and date all changes.)

_____

_____

_____

_____

_____

_____

_____

_____

_____

Family Member #2

Name: _____

HEALTH ALERTS

Health Alerts	
Date of Birth	
Blood Type	
Medication Allergies	
Food Allergies	

Additional Information & Updates: (Please be as specific as possible and date all changes.)

_____

_____

_____

_____

_____

_____

_____

_____

_____

_____

DIAGNOSES

Diagnosis		Diagnosis	
Year Diagnosed		Year Diagnosed	
Doctor		Doctor	
Surgery	Yes / No	Surgery	Yes / No
If yes, Date of Surgery		If yes, Date of Surgery	
Final Report Attached	Yes / No	Final Report Attached	Yes / No

Diagnosis		Diagnosis	
Year Diagnosed		Year Diagnosed	
Doctor		Doctor	
Surgery	Yes / No	Surgery	Yes / No
If yes, Date of Surgery		If yes, Date of Surgery	
Final Report Attached	Yes / No	Final Report Attached	Yes / No

Diagnosis	Diagnosis
Year Diagnosed	Year Diagnosed
Doctor	Doctor
Surgery Yes / No	Surgery Yes / No
If yes, Date of Surgery	If yes, Date of Surgery
Final Report Attached Yes / No	Final Report Attached Yes / No

Additional Information & Updates: (Please be as specific as possible and date all changes.)

_____

_____

_____

_____

_____

_____

_____

_____

_____

_____

MEDICATIONS

Medication Name	Medication Name
Dosage	Dosage
Route (*by mouth, injected, etc.*)	Route (*by mouth, injected, etc.*)
Frequency (*how often taken*)	Frequency (*how often taken*)
Indication (*reason for taking*)	Indication (*reason for taking*)
Prescribing Doctor	Prescribing Doctor

Medication Name	Medication Name
Dosage	Dosage
Route (*by mouth, injected, etc.*)	Route (*by mouth, injected, etc.*)
Frequency (*how often taken*)	Frequency (*how often taken*)
Indication (*reason for taking*)	Indication (*reason for taking*)
Prescribing Doctor	Prescribing Doctor

Medication Name	Medication Name
Dosage	Dosage
Route (*by mouth, injected, etc.*)	Route (*by mouth, injected, etc.*)
Frequency (*how often taken*)	Frequency (*how often taken*)
Indication (*reason for taking*)	Indication (*reason for taking*)
Prescribing Doctor	Prescribing Doctor

Medication Name	Medication Name
Dosage	Dosage
Route (*by mouth, injected, etc.*)	Route (*by mouth, injected, etc.*)
Frequency (*how often taken*)	Frequency (*how often taken*)
Indication (*reason for taking*)	Indication (*reason for taking*)
Prescribing Doctor	Prescribing Doctor

Medication Name	Medication Name
Dosage	Dosage
Route (*by mouth, injected, etc.*)	Route (*by mouth, injected, etc.*)
Frequency (*how often taken*)	Frequency (*how often taken*)
Indication (*reason for taking*)	Indication (*reason for taking*)
Prescribing Doctor	Prescribing Doctor

Additional Information & Updates: (Please be as specific as possible and date all changes.)

_____
_____
_____
_____
_____
_____
_____
_____
_____
_____
_____
_____

If you have received Durable Medical Equipment (DME) supplies or any assistive devices, be sure to itemize them below. *(Wheelchairs, hospital beds, walkers, oxygen, hearing aids, etc.)*

ASSISTIVE DEVICE	PRESCRIBING DOCTOR	DME SUPPLY COMPANY	PHONE #

Additional Information & Updates: (Please be as specific as possible and date all changes.)

_____

_____

_____

_____

_____

_____

_____

_____

3.2 HEALTH INSURANCE & PRESCRIPTION COVERAGE

PRIMARY INSURANCE

PRIMARY INSURANCE	FAMILY MEMBER #1	FAMILY MEMBER #2
Family Member Name		
Primary Insurance Company		
Primary Insurance Company #		
Policyholder Name		
Policyholder DOB		
Policyholder Employer Name		
Policy # (as it appears on card)		
Type of Coverage (circle one)	Individual / Family	Individual / Family
# of Dependents on Policy		
Health Insurance Premium	$	$
Premium Paid (circle one)	Wkly / Bi-Wkly / Mthly / Yearly	Wkly / Bi-Wkly / Mthly / Yearly
Deductible Amount	$	$
Copayment Due (outpatient)	$	$
Copayment Due (in-patient)	$	$
Copayment Due (hospital)	$	$
Hospital of Choice		
Hospital Choice (City/State)		
Primary Insurance Website		
Policyholder Portal Login		
Policyholder Portal Password		
Policyholder Portal Pin #		
Primary Insurance Address		
City		
State		
Zip Code		

DEPENDENTS (PRIMARY INSURANCE)

DEPENDENTS' NAMES AND DOB	DEPENDENTS' NAMES AND DOB
1.	4.
2.	5.
3.	6.

Additional Information & Updates: (Please be as specific as possible and date all changes.)

_____

_____

_____

_____

_____

_____

_____

_____

_____

_____

SECONDARY INSURANCE

PRIMARY INSURANCE	FAMILY MEMBER #1	FAMILY MEMBER #2
Family Member Name		
Primary Insurance Company		
Primary Insurance Company #		
Policyholder Name		
Policyholder DOB		
Policyholder Employer Name		
Policy # (*as it appears on card*)		
Type of Coverage (*circle one*)	Individual / Family	Individual / Family
# of Dependents on Policy		
Health Insurance Premium	$	$
Premium Paid (*circle one*)	Wkly / Bi-Wkly / Mthly / Yearly	Wkly / Bi-Wkly / Mthly / Yearly
Deductible Amount	$	$
Copayment Due (*outpatient*)	$	$
Copayment Due (*in-patient*)	$	$
Copayment Due (*hospital*)	$	$
Hospital of Choice		

Hospital Choice (*City/State*)		
Primary Insurance Website		
Policyholder Portal Login		
Policyholder Portal Password		
Policyholder Portal Pin #		
Primary Insurance Address		
City		
State		
Zip Code		

DEPENDENTS (SECONDARY INSURANCE)

DEPENDENTS' NAMES & DOB	DEPENDENTS' NAMES & DOB
1.	4.
2.	5.
3.	6.

Additional Information & Updates: (Please be as specific as possible and date all changes.)

_____

_____

_____

_____

_____

_____

_____

_____

_____

MEDICARE (PRIMARY INSURANCE)

MEDICARE PRIMARY INSURANCE	FAMILY MEMBER #1	FAMILY MEMBER #2
Family Member Name		
Medicare Insurance	Yes / No	Yes / No
Policyholder Name		
Policyholder DOB		
Policy # (as it appears on card)		
Type of Coverage (*circle all that apply*)	Part A / B / C / D	Part A / B / C / D
Medicare Insurance Premium	Part A $ Part B $ Part C $ Part D $	Part A $ Part B $ Part C $ Part D $
Premium Paid (*circle one*)	Wkly / Bi-Wkly / Mthly / Yearly	Wkly / Bi-Wkly / Mthly / Yearly
Deductible Amount	$	$
Copayment Due (*outpatient*)	$	$
Copayment Due (*in-patient*)	$	$
Copayment Due (*hospital stay*)	$	$
Hospital of Choice		
Hospital Choice (*City/State*)		
Medicare Website		
Medicare Portal Login		
Medicare Portal Password		
Portal Pin #		
Medicare Phone #		
Medicare Headquarters Address		
City		
State		
Zip Code		

MEDICARE SUPPLEMENTAL INSURANCE

For those enrolled, supplemental Medicare Insurance covers 20% of medical expenses not otherwise covered by traditional Medicare, and can vary by state.

MEDICARE SUPPLEMENTAL INSURANCE	FAMILY MEMBER #1	FAMILY MEMBER #2
Family Member Name		
Supplemental Insurance	Yes / No	Yes / No
Policyholder Name		
Policyholder DOB		
Policy # (as it appears on card)		
Type of Coverage	Part	Part
Supplemental Medicare Insurance Premium	$	$
Premium Paid (circle one)	Wkly / Bi-Wkly / Mthly /Yearly	Wkly / Bi-Wkly / Mthly / Yearly
Deductible Amount	$	$
Copayment Due (outpatient)	$	$
Copayment Due (in-patient)	$	$
Copayment Due (hospital stay)	$	$
Hospital of Choice		
Hospital of Choice (City/State)		
Supplemental Medicare Website		
Supplemental Medicare Portal Login		
Supplemental Medicare Portal Password		
Supplemental Portal Pin #		
Medicare #		
Supplemental Medicare Headquarters Address		
City		
State		
Zip Code		

Additional Information & Updates: (Please be as specific as possible and date all changes.)

_____

_____

_____

_____

_____

_____

_____

_____

_____

MEDICAID INSURANCE

MEDICAID INSURANCE	FAMILY MEMBER #1	FAMILY MEMBER #2
Family Member Name		
Medicaid Insurance	Yes / No	Yes / No
State of Issuance		
Local Medicaid Phone #		
Medicaid Caseworker Phone #		
Caseworker Cell Phone #		
Claims Department Phone #		
Claims Department Fax #		
Medicaid Identification (ID) #		
Medicaid Effective Date		
Medicaid Recertification Date		
Coverage Type (*Circle one*)	Community / Long-Term Care	Community / Long-Term Care
Pool Trust Amount Paid	$	$
Pool Trust Paid To: Name		
Pool Trust Company Phone #		
Did you apply for Medicaid on your own?	Yes / No	Yes / No
(If no) Firm/Agency who applied on your behalf		
Have your assets been placed in a trust?	Yes / No	Yes / No
Spousal Refusal	Yes / No	Yes / No
Attorney/Agent Name		
Attorney/Agent Office Phone #		
Attorney/Agent Cell Phone #		
Attorney/Agent Email Address		
Department of Social Services Website		

Client Portal Login		
Client Portal Password		
Client Portal Pin #		
Firm/Agency Company Address		
City		
State		
Zip Code		

Additional Information & Updates: (Please be as specific as possible and date all changes.)

_____
_____
_____
_____
_____
_____
_____
_____

PRESCRIPTION COVERAGE – PRIMARY (PHARMACY) INSURANCE

PRESCRIPTION COVERAGE - PRIMARY	FAMILY MEMBER #1	FAMILY MEMBER #2
Family Member Name		
Local Pharmacy Name		
Local Pharmacy Phone #		
Policyholder Name		
Policyholder DOB		
Policyholder Employer Name		
Policy # (as it appears on card)		
Prescription Tier # 1 Costs	$	$
Prescription Tier # 2 Costs	$	$
Prescription Tier # 3 Costs	$	$
Local Pharmacy Website		
Local Pharmacy Portal Login		
Local Pharmacy Portal Password		
Local Pharmacy Portal Pin #		
Local Pharmacy Address		

City		
State		
Zip Code		

Additional Information & Updates: (Please be as specific as possible and date all changes.)

_____

_____

_____

_____

_____

_____

_____

_____

_____

PRESCRIPTION COVERAGE – SECONDARY (PHARMACY) INSURANCE

PRESCRIPTION COVERAGE – SECONDARY	FAMILY MEMBER #1	FAMILY MEMBER #2
Family Member Name		
Local Pharmacy Name		
Local Pharmacy Phone #		
Policyholder Name		
Policyholder DOB		
Policyholder Employer Name		
Policy # (as it appears on card)		
Prescription Tier # 1 Costs	$	$
Prescription Tier # 2 Costs	$	$
Prescription Tier # 3 Costs	$	$
Local Pharmacy Website		
Local Pharmacy Portal Login		
Local Pharmacy Portal Password		
Local Pharmacy Portal Pin #		
Local Pharmacy Address		
City		
State		
Zip Code		

Additional Information & Updates: (Please be as specific as possible and date all changes.)

_____
_____
_____
_____
_____
_____
_____
_____
_____
_____

PRESCRIPTION COVERAGE – ONLINE (PHARMACY) DELIVERY COVERAGE

PRESCRIPTION COVERAGE – ONLINE	FAMILY MEMBER #1	FAMILY MEMBER #2
Family Member Name		
Online Pharmacy Name		
Online Pharmacy Phone #		
Policyholder Name		
Policyholder DOB		
Policyholder Employer Name		
Policy # (as it appears on card)		
Prescription Tier # 1 Costs	$	$
Prescription Tier # 2 Costs	$	$
Prescription Tier # 3 Costs	$	$
Online Pharmacy Website		
Online Pharmacy Portal Login		
Online Portal Password		
Online Pharmacy Portal Pin #		
Online Pharmacy Address		
City		
State		
Zip Code		

Additional Information & Updates: (Please be as specific as possible and date all changes.)

_____

_____

_____

_____

_____

_____

_____

_____

_____

3.3 PHYSICIANS & SERVICES

INTERNAL MEDICINE

INTERNAL MEDICINE	FAMILY MEMBER #1	FAMILY MEMBER #2
Family Member Name		
Doctor's Name		
Office Phone #		
Doctor's Cell Phone #		
Office Fax #		
Emergency Hotline #		
Office Email Address		
Office Website		
Patient Portal Login		
Patient Portal Password		
Patient Portal Pin #		
Doctor's Office Address		
City		
State		
Zip Code		
Billing Phone #		
Billing Address		
City		
State		
Zip Code		

Additional Information & Updates: (Please be as specific as possible and date all changes.)

_____

_____

_____

_____

_____

_____

_____

MEDICAL SPECIALISTS

Check below to indicate what types of **medical specialists** you visit, if any. Provide contact information for any specialist checked below.

Family Member #1

Name: _____

☐ **Anesthesiologist** ☐ Phone #	☐ **Gerontologist** ☐ Phone#	☐ **OBGYN** ☐ Phone #	☐ **Plastic Surgeon** ☐ Phone #
☐ **Cardiologist** ☐ Phone #	☐ **Hematologist** ☐ Phone #	☐ **Oncologist** ☐ Phone #	☐ **Podiatrist** ☐ Phone #
☐ **Dermatologist** ☐ Phone #	☐ **Immunologist** ☐ Phone #	☐ **Ophthalmologist** ☐ Phone #	☐ **Pulmonologist** ☐ Phone #
☐ **Endocrinologist** ☐ Phone #	☐ **Infectious Disease** ☐ Phone #	☐ **Orthopedic** ☐ Phone #	☐ **Rheumatologist** ☐ Phone #
☐ **Gastroenterologist** ☐ Phone #	☐ **Nephrologist** ☐ Phone #	☐ **Otolaryngologist (ENT)** ☐ Phone #	☐ **Urologist** ☐ Phone #
☐ **General Surgeon** ☐ Phone #	☐ **Neurologist** ☐ Phone #	☐ **Pathologist** ☐ Phone #	☐ **Other:** ☐ Phone #

Additional Information, Physician Contact Information & Updates: (Please be as specific as possible and date all changes.)

_____
_____
_____
_____
_____
_____
_____
_____

Family Member #2

Name: _____

☐ **Anesthesiologist**	☐ **Gerontologist**	☐ **OBGYN**	☐ **Plastic Surgeon**
☐ Phone #	☐ Phone#	☐ Phone #	☐ Phone #
☐ **Cardiologist**	☐ **Hematologist**	☐ **Oncologist**	☐ **Podiatrist**
☐ Phone #	☐ Phone #	☐ Phone #	☐ Phone #
☐ **Dermatologist**	☐ **Immunologist**	☐ **Ophthalmologist**	☐ **Pulmonologist**
☐ Phone #	☐ Phone #	☐ Phone #	☐ Phone #
☐ **Endocrinologist**	☐ **Infectious Disease**	☐ **Orthopedic**	☐ **Rheumatologist**
☐ Phone #	☐ Phone #	☐ Phone #	☐ Phone #
☐ **Gastroenterologist**	☐ **Nephrologist**	☐ **Otolaryngologist (ENT)**	☐ **Urologist**
☐ Phone #	☐ Phone #	☐ Phone #	☐ Phone #
☐ **General Surgeon**	☐ **Neurologist**	☐ **Pathologist**	☐ **Other:**
☐ Phone #	☐ Phone #	☐ Phone #	☐ Phone #

Additional Information, Physician Contact Information & Updates: (Please be as specific as possible and date all changes.)

_____

_____

_____

_____

_____

_____

_____

_____

_____

LABORATORY SERVICES

LABORATORY SERVICES	FAMILY MEMBER #1	FAMILY MEMBER #2
Family Member Name		
DOB		
Laboratory Company Name		
Laboratory Phone #		
Laboratory Fax #		
Laboratory Email Address		
Laboratory Website		
Laboratory Portal Login		
Laboratory Portal Password		
Laboratory Portal Pin #		
Laboratory Local Address		
City		
State		
Zip Code		
Laboratory Billing Phone #		
Laboratory Billing Fax #		
Laboratory Billing Address		
City		
State		
Zip Code		

Additional Information & Updates: (Please be as specific as possible and date all changes.)

_____

_____

_____

_____

_____

_____

_____

_____

_____

RADIOLOGY SERVICES

X-ray, MRI, CT Scan, Etc.

RADIOLOGY SERVICES	FAMILY MEMBER #1	FAMILY MEMBER #2
Family Member Name		
DOB		
Radiology Company Name		
Radiology Phone #		
Radiology Fax #		
Radiology Email Address		
Radiology Website		
Radiology Portal Login		
Radiology Portal Password		
Radiology Portal Pin #		
Radiology Local Address		
City		
State		
Zip Code		
Radiology Billing Phone #		
Radiology Billing Fax #		
Radiology Billing Address		
City		
State		
Zip Code		
Type of Service (*Check all that apply*)	☐ Bone Density Test	☐ Bone Density Test
	☐ Breast Biopsy	☐ Breast Biopsy
	☐ Breast Sonogram	☐ Breast Sonogram
	☐ CT Scan (CAT SCAN)	☐ CT Scan (CAT SCAN)
	☐ Mammogram	☐ Mammogram
	☐ MRI Scan	☐ MRI Scan
	☐ Ultrasound	☐ Ultrasound
	☐ Ultrasound Guided Procedure	☐ Ultrasound Guided Procedure
	☐ X-ray	☐ X-ray
	☐ Other:	☐ Other:
	☐ Other:	☐ Other:

Additional Information & Updates: (Please be as specific as possible and date all changes.)

_____

_____

_____

_____

_____

_____

_____

_____

_____

3.4 DENTAL COVERAGE & SERVICES

DENTAL INSURANCE COVERAGE

DENTAL INSURANCE COVERAGE	FAMILY MEMBER #1	FAMILY MEMBER #2
Family Member Name		
Dental Insurance Company		
Dental Insurance Phone #		
Dental Insurance Fax #		
Policyholder Name		
Policyholder DOB		
Policyholder Employer Name		
Policy # (as it appears on card)		
Type of Coverage (circle one)	Individual / Family	Individual / Family
# of Dependents on Policy		
Dental Insurance Premium	$	$
Premium Paid (circle one)	Wkly / Bi-Wkly / Mthly / Yearly	Wkly / Bi-Wkly / Mthly / Yearly
Deductible Amount	$	$
Hospital of Choice		
Hospital Choice (City/State)		
Dental Insurance Website		
Policyholder Portal Login		
Policyholder Portal Password		
Policyholder Portal Pin #		
Dental Insurance Address		
City		
State		
Zip Code		

Additional Information & Updates: (Please be as specific as possible and date all changes.)

_____

_____

_____

_____

_____
_____
_____
_____
_____

DENTIST

DENTIST	FAMILY MEMBER #1	FAMILY MEMBER #2
Family Member Name		
General Dentist/Doctor's Name		
Dentistry Type		
Dental Office Phone #		
Dentist Cell Phone #		
Dental Office Fax #		
Dental Email Address		
Dental Website		
Dental Portal Login		
Dental Portal Password		
Dental Portal Pin #		
Local Dentist Address		
City		
State		
Zip Code		

Additional Information & Updates: (Please be as specific as possible and date all changes.)

_____
_____
_____
_____
_____
_____
_____

DENTAL SPECIALISTS

Check below to indicate what types of dental **specialists** you visit, if any. Provide contact information for any specialist checked below.

Family Member #1

Name: _____

☐ **Endodontist**	☐ **Oral Surgeon**	☐ **Periodontist**
☐ Phone #	☐ Phone #	☐ Phone #
☐ **General Dentist**	☐ **Orthodontist**	☐ **Prosthodontist**
☐ Phone #	☐ Phone #	☐ Phone #

Family Member #2

Name: _____

☐ **Endodontist**	☐ **Oral Surgeon**	☐ **Periodontist**
☐ Phone #	☐ Phone #	☐ Phone #
☐ **General Dentist**	☐ **Orthodontist**	☐ **Prosthodontist**
☐ Phone #	☐ Phone #	☐ Phone #

Additional Information & Updates: (Please be as specific as possible and date all changes.)

_____
_____
_____
_____
_____
_____
_____
_____

3.5 VISION COVERAGE & SERVICES

VISION INSURANCE COVERAGE

VISION INSURANCE COVERAGE	FAMILY MEMBER #1	FAMILY MEMBER #2
Family Member Name		
Vision Insurance Company		
Vision Insurance Phone #		
Vision Insurance Fax #		
Policyholder Name		
Policyholder DOB		
Policyholder Employer Name		
Policy # (as it appears on card)		
Type of Coverage (circle one)	Individual / Family	Individual / Family
# of Dependents on Policy		
Vision Insurance Premium	$	$
Premium Paid (circle one)	Wkly / Bi-Wkly / Mthly / Yearly	Wkly / Bi-Wkly / Mthly / Yearly
Deductible Amount	$	$
Copayment Amount	$	$
Glasses	Max. Amount Allowed $	Max. Amount Allowed $
Contact Lens	Max. Amount Allowed $	Max. Amount Allowed $
Eligible for New Glasses/Lens	Every:	Every:
Hospital of Choice		
Hospital of Choice (City/State)		
Vision Insurance Website		
Vision Portal Login		
Vision Portal Password		
Vision Portal Pin #		
Vision Insurance Address		
City		
State		
Zip Code		

Additional Information & Updates: (Please be as specific as possible and date all changes.)

_____

_____

_____

_____

_____

_____

_____

_____

_____

_____

VISION SPECIALISTS

Check below to indicate what types of vision specialists you visit, if any. Provide contact information for any specialist checked below.

Family Member #1

Name: _____

☐ **Ophthalmologist**	☐ **Optician**	☐ **Optometrist**
☐ Phone #	☐ Phone #	☐ Phone #

Family Member #2

Name: _____

☐ **Ophthalmologist**	☐ **Optician**	☐ **Optometrist**
☐ Phone #	☐ Phone #	☐ Phone #

Additional Information & Updates: (Please be as specific as possible and date all changes.)

_____

_____

_____

_____

_____

_____

_____

_____

3.6 SPECIALTY MEDICAL COVERAGE & SERVICES

SPECIALTY MEDICAL COVERAGE

SPECIALTY MEDICAL COVERAGE	FAMILY MEMBER #1	FAMILY MEMBER #2
Family Member Name		
Policyholder Name		
Policyholder DOB		
Policyholder Employer Name		
Policy #		
Type of Coverage (Check all that apply)	☐ Cancer	☐ Cancer
	☐ Durable Medical Supplies	☐ Durable Medical Supplies
	☐ Home Care	☐ Home Care
	☐ Hospice	☐ Hospice
	☐ Infertility	☐ Infertility
	☐ Managed Health Care	☐ Managed Health Care
	☐ Mental Health Care	☐ Mental Health Care
	☐ Occupational Therapy	☐ Occupational Therapy
	☐ Physical Therapy	☐ Physical Therapy
	☐ Skilled Nursing	☐ Skilled Nursing
	☐ Speech Therapy	☐ Speech Therapy
	☐ Transplant	☐ Transplant
	☐ Other:	☐ Other:
	☐ Other:	☐ Other:

Additional Information & Updates: (Please be as specific as possible and date all changes.)

_____

_____

_____

_____

_____

_____

_____

LONG-TERM CARE INSURANCE

LONG-TERM CARE INSURANCE	FAMILY MEMBER #1	FAMILY MEMBER #2
Family Member Name		
Long-Term Care Coverage	Yes / No	Yes / No
Company Name		
Company Phone #		
Claims Department Phone #		
Claims Department Fax #		
Policy #		
Effective Date		
Coverage Type		
Premium Amount	$	$
Premium Paid (circle one)	Wkly / Bi-Wkly / Mthly / Yearly	Wkly / Bi-Wkly / Mthly / Yearly
State of Issuance		
Agent Phone #		
Agent Cell Phone #		
Agent Email Address		
Company Website		
Client Portal Login		
Client Portal Password		
Client Portal Pin #		
Company Address		
City		
State		
Zip Code		

Additional Information & Updates: (Please be as specific as possible and date all changes.)

_____
_____
_____
_____
_____

SHORT-TERM DISABILITY INSURANCE

SHORT-TERM DISABILITY INSURANCE	FAMILY MEMBER #1	FAMILY MEMBER #2
Family Member Name		
Short-Term Disability Coverage	Yes / No	Yes / No
Company Name		
Company Phone #		
Claims Department Phone #		
Claims Department Fax #		
Policy #		
Effective Date		
Coverage Type		
Premium Amount	$	$
Premium Paid (circle one)	Wkly / Bi-Wkly / Mthly / Yearly	Wkly / Bi-Wkly / Mthly / Yearly
State of Issuance		
Agent Phone #		
Agent Cell Phone #		
Agent Email Address		
Company Website		
Client Portal Login		
Client Portal Password		
Client Portal Pin #		
Company Address		
City		
State		
Zip Code		

Additional Information & Updates: (Please be as specific as possible and date all changes.)

_____
_____
_____

_____

_____

_____

_____

_____

_____

MEDICAL STORAGE

MEDICAL STORAGE	FAMILY MEMBER #1	FAMILY MEMBER #2
Family Member Name		
Storage Company Name		
Storage Company Phone #		
Storage Company Fax #		
Storage Company Email Address		
Storage Company Website		
Client Portal Login		
Client Portal Password		
Client Portal Pin #		
Client Security Passcode		
Contents Stored (*Check all that apply*)	☐ Blood (autologous blood)	☐ Blood (autologous blood)
	☐ Embryos	☐ Embryos
	☐ Ovum	☐ Ovum
	☐ Plasma	☐ Plasma
	☐ Platelets	☐ Platelets
	☐ Semen	☐ Semen
	☐ Umbilical Cord Blood	☐ Umbilical Cord Blood
	☐ Other:	☐ Other:
Date Collected		
Contents Collected By		
Hospital Name – Collection Site		
Hospital (*City and State*)		
Policy #/Account #		
Does Insurance Cover Service	Yes / No	Yes / No
Storage Coordinator Name		
Coordinator Office Phone #		
Coordinator Cell Phone #		

Coordinator Fax #		
Coordinator Email Address		
Do You Have Joint Ownership?	Yes / No	Yes / No
Recipient Name (If applicable)		
Recipient Phone #		
Recipient Cell Phone #		
Recipient Email Address		
Recipient Address		
City		
State		
Zip Code		
Recipient Emergency Contact Name		
Contact Phone #		
Contact Cell Phone #		
Contact Email Address		
Emergency Contact Address		
City		
State		
Zip Code		

Additional Information & Updates: (Please be as specific as possible and date all changes.)

_____

_____

_____

_____

_____

_____

_____

_____

_____

3.7 MENTAL HEALTH COVERAGE & SERVICES

MENTAL HEALTH INSURANCE COVERAGE

MENTAL HEALTH INSURANCE	FAMILY MEMBER #1	FAMILY MEMBER #2
Family Member Name		
Policyholder Name		
Policyholder DOB		
Company Name		
Company Phone #		
Company Fax #		
Policy #		
Copayment Amount	$	$
Deductible Amount	$	$
Company Email Address		
Company Website		
Company Portal Login		
Company Portal Password		
Company Portal Pin #		
Company Local Address		
City		
State		
Zip Code		
Company Billing Phone #		
Company Billing Address		
City		
State		
Zip Code		

Additional Information & Updates: (Please be as specific as possible and date all changes.)

_____

_____

_____

_____

_____

_____
_____
_____
_____
_____

PSYCHIATRIST

PSYCHIATRIST	FAMILY MEMBER #1	FAMILY MEMBER #2
Family Member Name		
DOB		
Business/Company Name		
Psychiatrist Name		
Office Phone #		
Office Fax #		
Psychiatrist Cell Phone #		
Emergency Hotline #		
Hospital Affiliation		
Office Email Address		
Website		
Patient Portal Login		
Patient Portal Password		
Patient Portal Pin #		
Psychiatrist Office Address		
City		
State		
Zip Code		
Psychiatrist Billing Phone #		
Psychiatrist Billing Address		
City		
State		
Zip Code		

Additional Information & Updates: (Please be as specific as possible and date all changes.)

_____
_____
_____

_____
_____
_____
_____
_____
_____

PSYCHOTHERAPIST

PSYCHOTHERAPIST	FAMILY MEMBER #1	FAMILY MEMBER #2
Family Member Name		
DOB		
Business/Company Name		
Therapist Name		
Office Phone #		
Office Fax #		
Therapist Cell Phone #		
Emergency Hotline #		
Hospital Affiliation		
Office Email Address		
Website		
Patient Portal Login		
Patient Portal Password		
Patient Portal Pin #		
Therapist Office Address		
City		
State		
Zip Code		
Therapist Billing Phone #		
Therapist Billing Address		
City		
State		
Zip Code		

Additional Information & Updates: (Please be as specific as possible and date all changes.)

_____
_____

_____
_____
_____
_____
_____
_____
_____
_____

MENTAL HEALTH TREATMENT FACILITY

MENTAL HEALTH TREATMENT FACILITY	FAMILY MEMBER #1	FAMILY MEMBER #2
Family Member Name		
DOB		
Treatment Facility Name		
Facility Main Phone #		
Emergency Hotline #		
Hospital Affiliation		
Does insurance cover services?	Yes / No	Yes / No
Admissions Director Name		
Admissions Phone #		
Admissions Cell Phone #		
Admissions Email Address		
Social Worker's Name		
Social Worker's Phone #		
Social Worker's Cell Phone #		
Social Worker's Email Address		
Treatment Facility Website		
Patient Portal Login		
Patient Portal Password		
Patient Portal Pin #		
Patient Security Passcode		
Facility Treatment Address		
City		
State		
Zip Code		
Facility Billing Phone #		
Facility Billing Address		

City		
State		
Zip Code		

Additional Information & Updates: (Please be as specific as possible and date all changes.)

_____

_____

_____

_____

_____

_____

_____

_____

_____

_____

SUBSTANCE ABUSE TREATMENT FACILITY

SUBSTANCE ABUSE TREATMENT FACILITY	FAMILY MEMBER #1	FAMILY MEMBER #2
Family Member Name		
DOB		
Treatment Facility Name		
Facility Main Phone #		
Emergency Hotline #		
Hospital Affiliation		
Does insurance cover services?	Yes / No	Yes / No
Admissions Director Name		
Admissions Phone #		
Admission Cell Phone #		
Admissions Email Address		
Counselor's Name		
Counselor's Phone #		
Counselor's Cell Phone #		
Counselor Email Address		
Social Worker's Name		
Social Worker's Phone #		
Social Worker's Cell Phone #		

Social Worker's Email Address		
Credentialed Alcoholism and Substance Abuse Counselor Name		
CASAC Counselor Phone #		
CASAC Counselor Cell Phone#		
CASAC Counselor Email Address		
Sponsor's Name		
Sponsor's Cell Phone #		
Sponsor's Email Address		
Treatment Facility Website		
Patient Portal Login		
Patient Portal Password		
Patient Portal Pin #		
Patient Security Passcode		
Treatment Facility Address		
City		
State		
Zip Code		
Facility Billing Phone #		
Facility Billing Address		
City		
State		
Zip Code		
Alcoholics Anonymous (AA) Name		
AA Coordinator's Office #		
AA Coordinator Cell Phone #		
AA Day/Hour of Meeting		
AA Location Address		
City		
State		
Zip Code		

Additional Information & Updates: (Please be as specific as possible and date all changes.)

_____

_____

_____
_____
_____
_____
_____
_____
_____
_____

HEALTH & MEDICAL PROFILE DOCUMENT CHECKLIST

Include a copy or originals of the following documents with your *Life Management Portfolio: A How-To-Guide for Organizing Your Life*.

Health Insurance & Prescription Coverage:

☐ Health Insurance Card(s) – Primary and Secondary (front and back)

☐ Medicare Card (front and back)

☐ Medicare Supplemental Insurance Card (front and back)

☐ Medicaid Card (front and back)

☐ Prescription Drug Coverage Card, (if applicable, front and back)

☐ Post a list of medication in your kitchen

☐ Durable Medical Equipment (DME) supply list

Physicians & Services:

☐ Added contact information for all medical specialists that were checked in corresponding areas

☐ Recent Lab Reports (i.e. genetics testing, confirmation of disorders/diagnosis)

☐ Recent Radiology Reports/Films

☐ Recent diagnostic testing results

☐ Latest hospital discharge paperwork *(if applicable)*

☐ Discuss Health Insurance Portability and Accountability Act (HIPAA) Authorization Form with doctors

Dental & Vision Coverage & Services:

☐ Dental Insurance Card (front and back)

☐ Vision Insurance Card (front and back)

Specialty Medical Coverage & Services:

☐ Proof of Specialty Coverage from your Benefits Administrator outlining all services included

☐ Long-Term Care Insurance Policy

☐ Short-Term Disability Insurance Policy

☐ Medical Storage Contract *(if applicable)*

☐ Court reports outlining custody of Ovum, Embryos, Semen, Umbilical Cord Blood *(if applicable)*

Mental Health Coverage & Services:

☐ Mental Health/Substance Abuse Coverage outlining services included

☐ Latest facility discharge paperwork *(if applicable)*

Notes - Explanation for items left unchecked:

_____

_____

_____

_____

_____

_____

_____

_____

_____

_____

4.
CHILDREN & DEPENDENTS

Anyone who is a parent will know what I mean when I say, we do everything for our children. We make decisions for them, set their daily routines, anticipate their needs and make sure those needs are met. But we also do everything for our children in the sense that they become our reason for doing things. It's for their sake that we maintain a stable household, raise our families by certain principles, look ahead to the future—and make a plan for when things go awry.

This section of the workbook is invaluable, whether you are part of a two-parent household or a single parent raising your kids alone. Every parent holds certain parts of the household as his or her sole domain, so a resource like *The Life Management Profile: A How-To-Guide for Organizing Your Life* becomes essential in case anyone needs to step in to maintain your children's daily routines and provide them stability and continuity in the household. The conversation of who that person will be, who takes on guardianship, is also something you will explore with your family in this section.

 In this section, you will gather information regarding the following areas:

GUARDIANSHIP – The question of who will care for your minor children in your absence is a conversation to have with other adults in the home, but also a question to talk to your children about. Give them a voice in the discussion. Don't simply assume your choice of guardian will necessarily be the best person to care for your children; they may quickly let you know they prefer to be in the care of someone else.

CHILD(REN)'S PROFILE — Children find comfort in stability, especially in the midst of a crisis. This section asks you to provide some general information about each child, including where they go to school, what daily routines they follow, and what their world looks like, so that your children's routine will remain stable and unchanged, even if you are not there to care for them yourself.

CHILD(REN)'S HEALTH & MEDICAL PROFILE — Children, especially young ones, are not likely to have a full understanding of their medical profiles. It's therefore important for you, the adult, to provide a snapshot of your child's medical history should it ever be needed. Use this as an opportunity to talk with your children about their medical history as well, so they, too, can be well informed.

*NOTE: For information on child(ren)'s health and medical insurance coverage, refer back to Section 3.2, Health Insurance & Prescription Coverage.

PERSONS WITH DISABILITIES OR SPECIAL NEEDS — A huge amount of knowledge and care goes into managing the day-to-day activities for persons with disabilities or special needs. Provide as much information as possible within these workbook pages and include any and as much additional information as you think necessary to ensure their care will continue as planned.

CHILD(REN)'S FINANCIAL PROFILE — As parents, it's great to educate children in financial literacy to better plan for their financial future. Tracking these accounts here is important for protecting these investments and maintaining minor children's accounts.

HELPFUL TIPS

#1 Invite your children's input when exploring guardianship options.

#2 Your designated guardian and children should be aware of your *Life Management Portfolio: A How-To-Guide for Organizing Your Life* and its location.

#3 You can appoint a guardian in your will to avoid conflict or confusion – hence the need for one!

#4 School emergency contacts must be kept up-to-date. Educate your children on who their emergency contacts are.

#5 Educational profiles are helpful to those responsible for getting kids to and from school, and for informing school officials of changes within the home.

#6 Teach, educate and communicate with your children about stranger danger. This includes family members!

#7 Every family should have a safe word that alerts to danger.

#8 Check in with your children. You never know what may be causing your children stress or anxiety until you talk to them about their worries and how you can together come up with solutions and plans to alleviate them. This workbook is more than just a fill-in-the-blanks exercise; it's a chance for you to open some important discussions and tighten relationships.

4.1 GUARDIANSHIP

GUARDIANSHIP	FAMILY MEMBER #1	FAMILY MEMBER #2
Family Member Name		
Do you and your spouse/partner agree on who should care for the children in case of emergency?	Yes / No (*If no, start talking and exploring options*)	Yes / No (*If no, start talking and exploring options*)
Do you have a Trust Fund set up?	Yes / No	Yes / No
(*If yes*) Date Last Reviewed		
(*If no*) Have you explored the option of a Trust Fund?	Yes / No	Yes / No
Have you established guardianship legally?	Yes / No	Yes / No
(*If yes*) How was guardianship established?	Courts / Living Will / Trust / Other:	Courts / Living Will / Trust / Other:
Is your document notarized?	Yes / No (*If no, it may be invalid*)	Yes / No (*If no, it may be invalid*)
Who drafted the document?	Attorney / Courts / Other:	Attorney / Courts / Other:
State the person's name		
Office Phone #		
Cell Phone #		
Email Address		
Address		
City		
State		
Zip Code		
Is your guardian still alive?	Yes / No (*If no, you may need to make some revisions*)	Yes / No (*If no, you may need to make some revisions*)
Do you need to make changes?	Yes / No (*If yes, do so ASAP*)	Yes / No (*If yes, do so ASAP*)
Designated Guardian's Name		
Relationship to Child(ren)		
Designated Guardian's Phone #		
Designated Guardian's Cell Phone #		
Designated Guardian's Email Address		
Designated Guardian's Business Phone #		
Designated Guardian's Business Email Address		

Guardian's Address		
City		
State		
Zip Code		
Is there an alternate guardian?	Yes / No	Yes / No
Is the alternate guardian alive?	Yes / No (*If no, you may need to make some revisions*)	Yes / No (*If no, you may need to make some revisions*)
Do you need to make changes?	Yes / No (*If yes, do so ASAP*)	Yes / No (*If yes, do so ASAP*)
Alternate Guardian's Name		
Relationship to Child(ren)		
Alternate Guardian's Phone #		
Alternate Guardian's Cell Phone #		
Alternate Guardian's Email Address		
Alternate Guardian's Business Phone #		
Alternate Guardian's Business Email Address		
Alternate Guardian's Address		
City		
State		
Zip Code		

Additional Information & Updates: (Please be as specific as possible and date all changes.)

_____

_____

_____

_____

_____

_____

_____

_____

_____

4.2 CHILD(REN)'S PROFILE

CHILD(REN)'S PROFILE (#1)

Child's Full Name: _____

Date of Birth: _____

BAPTISMAL/CHRISTENING PROFILE	
Date of Baptismal/Christening	
Name of Officiant	
Name of Church/Venue	
Church Office Phone #	
Church/Venue Website	
Church/Venue Address	
City	
State	
Zip Code	

GODPARENTS	
Full Name	**Cell Phone #**
1.	
2.	
3.	

EDUCATIONAL PROFILE	
Name of Child's School	
School Main Phone #	
School District Main Phone #	
Guidance Counselor's Name	
Guidance Counselor's Phone #	
Guidance Counselor's Email Address	
School Social Worker's Name	
Social Worker's Phone #	
Social Worker's Email Address	
School Nurse's Name	

Nurse's Phone #	
Nurse's Email Address	
School Principal's Name	
Principal's Phone #	
Principal's Email Address	
Superintendent's Name	
Superintendent's Phone #	
Superintendent's Email Address	
School Website	
Student Portal Login	
Student Portal Password	
Student Portal Pin #	
Student Portal Passcode	
Parent Portal Login	
Parent Portal Password	
Parent Portal Pin #	
Parent Portal Passcode	
School Address	
City	
State	
Zip Code	

COLLEGE/UNIVERSITY	
Is your child enrolled in college?	Yes / No
Name of College/University	
Student's Cell Phone #	
Does student have a Durable Power of Attorney for Health Care (*if 18 years or older*)	Yes / No
Dorm Name (*if applicable*)	
Student's Dorm Address at School	
City, State & Zip Code	

SCHOOL EMERGENCY CONTACTS	
Full Name	**Cell Phone #**
1.	
2.	
3.	
4.	

Additional Information & Updates: (Please be as specific as possible and date all changes.)

_____
_____
_____
_____
_____
_____
_____
_____
_____
_____

CHILD(REN)'S PROFILE (#2)

Child's Full Name: _____

Date of Birth: _____

BAPTISMAL/CHRISTENING PROFILE	
Date of Baptismal/Christening	
Name of Officiant	
Name of Church/Venue	
Church Office Phone #	
Church/Venue Website	
Church/Venue Address	
City	
State	
Zip Code	

GODPARENTS	
Full Name	**Cell Phone #**
1.	
2.	
3.	

EDUCATIONAL PROFILE	
Name of Child's School	

School Main Phone #	
School District Main Phone #	
Guidance Counselor's Name	
Guidance Counselor's Phone #	
Guidance Counselor's Email Address	
School Social Worker's Name	
Social Worker's Phone #	
Social Worker's Email Address	
School Nurse's Name	
Nurse's Phone #	
Nurse's Email Address	
School Principal's Name	
Principal's Phone #	
Principal's Email Address	
Superintendent's Name	
Superintendent's Phone #	
Superintendent's Email Address	
School Website	
Student Portal Login	
Student Portal Password	
Student Portal Pin #	
Student Portal Passcode	
Parent Portal Login	
Parent Portal Password	
Parent Portal Pin #	
Parent Portal Passcode	
School Address	
City	
State	
Zip Code	

COLLEGE/UNIVERSITY	
Is your child enrolled in college?	Yes / No
Name of College/University	
Student's Cell Phone #	
Does student have a Durable Power of Attorney for Health Care (*if 18 years or older*)	Yes / No
Dorm Name (*if applicable*)	

Student's Dorm Address at School	
City, State & Zip Code	

SCHOOL EMERGENCY CONTACTS	
Full Name	**Cell Phone #**
1.	
2.	
3.	
4.	

Additional Information & Updates: (Please be as specific as possible and date all changes.)

_____

_____

_____

_____

_____

_____

_____

_____

_____

_____

_____

_____

CHILD(REN)'S PROFILE (#3)

Child's Full Name: _____

Date of Birth: _____

BAPTISMAL/CHRISTENING PROFILE	
Date of Baptismal/Christening	
Name of Officiant	
Name of Church/Venue	
Church Office Phone #	
Church/Venue Website	
Church/Venue Address	
City	
State	

Zip Code	

GODPARENTS	
Full Name	**Cell Phone #**
1.	
2.	
3.	

EDUCATIONAL PROFILE	
Name of Child's School	
School Main Phone #	
School District Main Phone #	
Guidance Counselor's Name	
Guidance Counselor's Phone #	
Guidance Counselor's Email Address	
School Social Worker's Name	
Social Worker's Phone #	
Social Worker's Email Address	
School Nurse's Name	
Nurse's Phone #	
Nurse's Email Address	
School Principal's Name	
Principal's Phone #	
Principal's Email Address	
Superintendent's Name	
Superintendent's Phone #	
Superintendent's Email Address	
School Website	
Student Portal Login	
Student Portal Password	
Student Portal Pin #	
Student Portal Passcode	
Parent Portal Login	
Parent Portal Password	
Parent Portal Pin #	
Parent Portal Passcode	
School Address	
City	

State	
Zip Code	

COLLEGE/UNIVERSITY	
Is your child enrolled in college?	Yes / No
Name of College/University	
Student's Cell Phone #	
Does student have a Durable Power of Attorney for Health Care *(if 18 years or older)*	Yes / No
Dorm Name *(if applicable)*	
Student's Dorm Address at School	
City, State & Zip Code	

SCHOOL EMERGENCY CONTACTS	
Full Name	**Cell Phone #**
1.	
2.	
3.	
4.	

Additional Information & Updates: (Please be as specific as possible and date all changes.)

_____

_____

_____

_____

_____

_____

_____

_____

_____

CHILD(REN)'S PROFILE (#4)

Child's Full Name: _____

Date of Birth: _____

BAPTISMAL/CHRISTENING PROFILE	
Date of Baptismal/Christening	
Name of Officiant	
Name of Church/Venue	
Church Office Phone #	
Church/Venue Website	
Church/Venue Address	
City	
State	
Zip Code	

GODPARENTS	
Full Name	**Cell Phone #**
1.	
2.	
3.	

EDUCATIONAL PROFILE	
Name of Child's School	
School Main Phone #	
School District Main Phone #	
Guidance Counselor's Name	
Guidance Counselor's Phone #	
Guidance Counselor's Email Address	
School Social Worker's Name	
Social Worker's Phone #	
Social Worker's Email Address	
School Nurse's Name	
Nurse's Phone #	
Nurse's Email Address	
School Principal's Name	
Principal's Phone #	
Principal's Email Address	

Superintendent's Name	
Superintendent's Phone #	
Superintendent's Email Address	
School Website	
Student Portal Login	
Student Portal Password	
Student Portal Pin #	
Student Portal Passcode	
Parent Portal Login	
Parent Portal Password	
Parent Portal Pin #	
Parent Portal Passcode	
School Address	
City	
State	
Zip Code	

COLLEGE/UNIVERSITY	
Is your child enrolled in college?	Yes / No
Name of College/University	
Student's Cell Phone #	
Does student have a Durable Power of Attorney for Health Care (if 18 years or older)	Yes / No
Dorm Name (if applicable)	
Student's Dorm Address at School	
City, State & Zip Code	

SCHOOL EMERGENCY CONTACTS	
Full Name	**Cell Phone #**
1.	
2.	
3.	
4.	

Additional Information & Updates: (Please be as specific as possible and date all changes.)

_____

_____
_____
_____
_____
_____
_____
_____
_____
_____

CHILD(REN)'S PROFILE (#5)

Child's Full Name: _____

Date of Birth: _____

BAPTISMAL/CHRISTENING PROFILE	
Date of Baptismal/Christening	
Name of Officiant	
Name of Church/Venue	
Church Office Phone #	
Church/Venue Website	
Church/Venue Address	
City	
State	
Zip Code	

GODPARENTS	
Full Name	**Cell Phone #**
1.	
2.	
3.	

EDUCATIONAL PROFILE	
Name of Child's School	
School Main Phone #	
School District Main Phone #	
Guidance Counselor's Name	
Guidance Counselor's Phone #	

Guidance Counselor's Email Address	
School Social Worker's Name	
Social Worker's Phone #	
Social Worker's Email Address	
School Nurse's Name	
Nurse's Phone #	
Nurse's Email Address	
School Principal's Name	
Principal's Phone #	
Principal's Email Address	
Superintendent's Name	
Superintendent's Phone #	
Superintendent's Email Address	
School Website	
Student Portal Login	
Student Portal Password	
Student Portal Pin #	
Student Portal Passcode	
Parent Portal Login	
Parent Portal Password	
Parent Portal Pin #	
Parent Portal Passcode	
School Address	
City	
State	
Zip Code	

COLLEGE/UNIVERSITY	
Is your child enrolled in college?	Yes / No
Name of College/University	
Student's Cell Phone #	
Does student have a Durable Power of Attorney for Health Care (*if 18 years or older*)	Yes / No
Dorm Name (*if applicable*)	
Student's Dorm Address at School	
City, State & Zip Code	

SCHOOL EMERGENCY CONTACTS	
Full Name	Cell Phone #
1.	
2.	
3.	
4.	

Additional Information & Updates: (Please be as specific as possible and date all changes.)

_____

_____

_____

_____

_____

_____

_____

_____

_____

_____

_____

CHILD(REN)'S PROFILE (#6)

Child's Full Name: _____

Date of Birth: _____

BAPTISMAL/CHRISTENING PROFILE	
Date of Baptismal/Christening	
Name of Officiant	
Name of Church/Venue	
Church Office Phone #	
Church/Venue Website	
Church/Venue Address	
City	
State	
Zip Code	

GODPARENTS	
Full Name	**Cell Phone #**
1.	
2.	
3.	

EDUCATIONAL PROFILE	
Name of Child's School	
School Main Phone #	
School District Main Phone #	
Guidance Counselor's Name	
Guidance Counselor's Phone #	
Guidance Counselor's Email Address	
School Social Worker's Name	
Social Worker's Phone #	
Social Worker's Email Address	
School Nurse's Name	
Nurse's Phone #	
Nurse's Email Address	
School Principal's Name	
Principal's Phone #	
Principal's Email Address	
Superintendent's Name	
Superintendent's Phone #	
Superintendent's Email Address	
School Website	
Student Portal Login	
Student Portal Password	
Student Portal Pin #	
Student Portal Passcode	
Parent Portal Login	
Parent Portal Password	
Parent Portal Pin #	
Parent Portal Passcode	
School Address	
City	
State	
Zip Code	

COLLEGE/UNIVERSITY	
Is your child enrolled in college?	Yes / No
Name of College/University	
Student's Cell Phone #	
Does student have a Durable Power of Attorney for Health Care *(if 18 years or older)*	Yes / No
Dorm Name *(if applicable)*	
Student's Dorm Address at School	
City, State & Zip Code	

SCHOOL EMERGENCY CONTACTS	
Full Name	**Cell Phone #**
1.	
2.	
3.	
4.	

Additional Information & Updates: (Please be as specific as possible and date all changes.)

_____
_____
_____
_____
_____
_____
_____
_____
_____
_____
_____

4.3 CHILD(REN)'S HEALTH & MEDICAL PROFILE

CHILD(REN)'S HEALTH & MEDICAL PROFILE (#1)

Child's Full Name: _____

Date of Birth: _____

HEALTH ALERTS

HEALTH ALERTS	
Blood Type	
Medication Allergies	
Food Allergies	
Other	

Additional Information & Updates: (Please be as specific as possible and date all changes.)

_____

_____

_____

_____

_____

_____

_____

_____

_____

DIAGNOSIS

Diagnosis		Diagnosis	
Year Diagnosed		Year Diagnosed	
Doctor		Doctor	
Surgery	Yes / No	Surgery	Yes / No
If yes, Date of Surgery		If yes, Date of Surgery	
Final Report Attached	Yes / No	Final Report Attached	Yes / No

Diagnosis		Diagnosis	
Year Diagnosed		Year Diagnosed	
Doctor		Doctor	
Surgery	Yes / No	Surgery	Yes / No
If yes, Date of Surgery		If yes, Date of Surgery	
Final Report Attached	Yes / No	Final Report Attached	Yes / No

Additional Information & Updates: (Please be as specific as possible and date all changes.)

_____
_____
_____
_____
_____
_____
_____
_____
_____
_____

MEDICATIONS

PHARMACY NAME	PHONE #

Medication Name		Medication Name	
Dosage		Dosage	
Route (by mouth, injected, etc.)		Route (by mouth, injected, etc.)	
Frequency (how often taken)		Frequency (how often taken)	
Indication (reason for taking)		Indication (reason for taking)	
Prescribing Doctor		Prescribing Doctor	

Medication Name		Medication Name	
Dosage		Dosage	
Route (by mouth, injected, etc.)		Route (by mouth, injected, etc.)	
Frequency (how often taken)		Frequency (how often taken)	
Indication (reason for taking)		Indication (reason for taking)	
Prescribing Doctor		Prescribing Doctor	

Medication Name	Medication Name

Dosage	Dosage
Route (*by mouth, injected, etc.*)	Route (*by mouth, injected, etc.*)
Frequency (*how often taken*)	Frequency (*how often taken*)
Indication (*reason for taking*)	Indication (*reason for taking*)
Prescribing Doctor	Prescribing Doctor

Additional Information & Updates: (Please be as specific as possible and date all changes.)

_____

_____

_____

_____

_____

_____

_____

_____

_____

_____

If you have received Durable Medical Equipment (DME) supplies or any assistive devices, be sure to itemize them below. *(Wheelchairs, hospital beds, walkers, oxygen, hearing aids, etc.)*

ASSISTIVE DEVICE	PRESCRIBING DOCTOR	DME SUPPLY COMPANY	PHONE #

Additional Information & Updates: (Please be as specific as possible and date all changes.)

_____

_____

_____

_____

_____

_____
_____
_____
_____

PEDIATRICIAN

PEDIATRICIAN	
Doctor's Name	
Doctor's Office Phone #	
Doctor's Cell Phone #	
Doctor's Office Fax #	
Emergency Hotline #	
Doctor's Office Email Address	
Doctor's Office Website	
Patient Portal Login	
Patient Portal Password	
Patient Portal Pin #	
Doctor's Office Address	
City	
State	
Zip Code	
Billing Phone #	
Billing Address	
City	
State	
Zip Code	

Additional Information & Updates: (Please be as specific as possible and date all changes.)

_____
_____
_____
_____
_____
_____
_____
_____
_____

MEDICAL SPECIALISTS

Check below to indicate what types of medical **specialists** your child utilizes, if any. Provide contact information for any specialist checked below.

☐ **Audiologist**	☐ **Infectious Disease**	☐ **Ophthalmologist**	☐ **Psychiatrist**
☐ Phone #	☐ Phone #	☐ Phone #	☐ Phone #
☐ **Cardiologist**	☐ **Mental Health**	☐ **Optician**	☐ **Psychotherapist**
☐ Phone #	☐ Phone #	☐ Phone #	☐ Phone #
☐ **Dentist**	☐ **Neonatologist**	☐ **Orthodontist**	☐ **Pulmonologist**
☐ Phone #	☐ Phone #	☐ Phone #	☐ Phone #
☐ **Dermatologist**	☐ **Nephrologist**	☐ **Orthopedic**	☐ **Rheumatologist**
☐ Phone #	☐ Phone #	☐ Phone #	☐ Phone #
☐ **Endocrinologist**	☐ **Neurologist**	☐ **Otolaryngologist (ENT)**	☐ **Speech Therapist**
☐ Phone #	☐ Phone #	☐ Phone #	☐ Phone #
☐ **Gastroenterologist**	☐ **Nutritionist**	☐ **Pathologist**	☐ **Substance Abuse**
☐ Phone #	☐ Phone #	☐ Phone #	☐ Phone #
☐ **General Surgeon**	☐ **OBGYN**	☐ **Physical Therapist**	☐ **Urologist**
☐ Phone #	☐ Phone #	☐ Phone #	☐ Phone #
☐ **Hematologist**	☐ **Occupational Therapist**	☐ **Plastic Surgeon**	☐ **Other:**
☐ Phone #	☐ Phone #	☐ Phone #	☐ Phone #
☐ **Immunologist**	☐ **Oncologist**	☐ **Podiatrist**	☐ **Other:**
☐ Phone #	☐ Phone #	☐ Phone #	☐ Phone #

Additional Information, Physician Contact Information & Updates: (Please be as specific as possible and date all changes.)

_____

_____

_____

_____

_____

_____

_____

_____

CHILD(REN)'S HEALTH & MEDICAL PROFILE (#2)

Child's Full Name: _____

Date of Birth: _____

HEALTH ALERTS

HEALTH ALERTS	
Blood Type	
Medication Allergies	
Food Allergies	
Other	

Additional Information & Updates: (Please be as specific as possible and date all changes.)

_____
_____
_____
_____
_____
_____
_____
_____
_____

DIAGNOSIS

Diagnosis		Diagnosis	
Year Diagnosed		Year Diagnosed	
Doctor		Doctor	
Surgery	Yes / No	Surgery	Yes / No
If yes, Date of Surgery		If yes, Date of Surgery	
Final Report Attached	Yes / No	Final Report Attached	Yes / No

Diagnosis		Diagnosis	
Year Diagnosed		Year Diagnosed	
Doctor		Doctor	
Surgery	Yes / No	Surgery	Yes / No
If yes, Date of Surgery		If yes, Date of Surgery	
Final Report Attached	Yes / No	Final Report Attached	Yes / No

Additional Information & Updates: (Please be as specific as possible and date all changes.)

_____

_____

_____

_____

_____

_____

_____

_____

_____

_____

MEDICATIONS

PHARMACY NAME	PHONE #

Medication Name	Medication Name
Dosage	Dosage
Route (*by mouth, injected, etc.*)	Route (*by mouth, injected, etc.*)
Frequency (*how often taken*)	Frequency (*how often taken*)
Indication (*reason for taking*)	Indication (*reason for taking*)
Prescribing Doctor	Prescribing Doctor

Medication Name	Medication Name
Dosage	Dosage
Route (*by mouth, injected, etc.*)	Route (*by mouth, injected, etc.*)
Frequency (*how often taken*)	Frequency (*how often taken*)
Indication (*reason for taking*)	Indication (*reason for taking*)
Prescribing Doctor	Prescribing Doctor

Medication Name	Medication Name
Dosage	Dosage
Route (*by mouth, injected, etc.*)	Route (*by mouth, injected, etc.*)
Frequency (*how often taken*)	Frequency (*how often taken*)
Indication (*reason for taking*)	Indication (*reason for taking*)
Prescribing Doctor	Prescribing Doctor

Additional Information & Updates: (Please be as specific as possible and date all changes.)

_____
_____
_____
_____
_____
_____
_____
_____
_____
_____

If you have received Durable Medical Equipment (DME) supplies or any assistive devices, be sure to itemize them below. *(Wheelchairs, hospital beds, walkers, oxygen, hearing aids, etc.)*

ASSISTIVE DEVICE	PRESCRIBING DOCTOR	DME SUPPLY COMPANY	PHONE #

Additional Information & Updates: (Please be as specific as possible and date all changes.)

_____
_____
_____
_____
_____
_____
_____
_____
_____

PEDIATRICIAN

PEDIATRICIAN	
Doctor's Name	
Doctor's Office Phone #	
Doctor's Cell Phone #	
Doctor's Office Fax #	
Emergency Hotline #	
Doctor's Office Email Address	
Doctor's Office Website	
Patient Portal Login	
Patient Portal Password	
Patient Portal Pin #	
Doctor's Office Address	
City	
State	
Zip Code	
Billing Phone #	
Billing Address	
City	
State	
Zip Code	

Additional Information & Updates: (Please be as specific as possible and date all changes.)

_____
_____
_____
_____
_____
_____
_____
_____
_____
_____

MEDICAL SPECIALISTS

Check below to indicate what types of medical **specialists** your child utilizes, if any. Provide contact information for any specialist checked below.

☐ **Audiologist**	☐ **Infectious Disease**	☐ **Ophthalmologist**	☐ **Psychiatrist**
☐ Phone #	☐ Phone #	☐ Phone #	☐ Phone #
☐ **Cardiologist**	☐ **Mental Health**	☐ **Optician**	☐ **Psychotherapist**
☐ Phone #	☐ Phone #	☐ Phone #	☐ Phone #
☐ **Dentist**	☐ **Neonatologist**	☐ **Orthodontist**	☐ **Pulmonologist**
☐ Phone #	☐ Phone #	☐ Phone #	☐ Phone #
☐ **Dermatologist**	☐ **Nephrologist**	☐ **Orthopedic**	☐ **Rheumatologist**
☐ Phone #	☐ Phone #	☐ Phone #	☐ Phone #
☐ **Endocrinologist**	☐ **Neurologist**	☐ **Otolaryngologist (ENT)**	☐ **Speech Therapist**
☐ Phone #	☐ Phone #	☐ Phone #	☐ Phone #
☐ **Gastroenterologist**	☐ **Nutritionist**	☐ **Pathologist**	☐ **Substance Abuse**
☐ Phone #	☐ Phone #	☐ Phone #	☐ Phone #
☐ **General Surgeon**	☐ **OBGYN**	☐ **Physical Therapist**	☐ **Urologist**
☐ Phone #	☐ Phone #	☐ Phone #	☐ Phone #
☐ **Hematologist**	☐ **Occupational Therapist**	☐ **Plastic Surgeon**	☐ **Other:**
☐ Phone #	☐ Phone #	☐ Phone #	☐ Phone #
☐ **Immunologist**	☐ **Oncologist**	☐ **Podiatrist**	☐ **Other:**
☐ Phone #	☐ Phone #	☐ Phone #	☐ Phone #

Additional Information, Physician Contact Information & Updates: (Please be as specific as possible and date all changes.)

_____

_____

_____

_____

_____

_____

_____

_____

_____

CHILD(REN)'S HEALTH & MEDICAL PROFILE (#3)

Child's Full Name: _____

Date of Birth: _____

HEALTH ALERTS

HEALTH ALERTS	
Blood Type	
Medication Allergies	
Food Allergies	
Other	

Additional Information & Updates: (Please be as specific as possible and date all changes.)

_____

_____

_____

_____

_____

_____

_____

_____

_____

DIAGNOSIS

Diagnosis		Diagnosis	
Year Diagnosed		Year Diagnosed	
Doctor		Doctor	
Surgery	Yes / No	Surgery	Yes / No
If yes, Date of Surgery		If yes, Date of Surgery	
Final Report Attached	Yes / No	Final Report Attached	Yes / No

Diagnosis		Diagnosis	
Year Diagnosed		Year Diagnosed	
Doctor		Doctor	
Surgery	Yes / No	Surgery	Yes / No
If yes, Date of Surgery		If yes, Date of Surgery	
Final Report Attached	Yes / No	Final Report Attached	Yes / No

Additional Information & Updates: (Please be as specific as possible and date all changes.)

_____

_____

_____

_____

_____

_____

_____

_____

_____

_____

MEDICATIONS

PHARMACY NAME	PHONE #

Medication Name	Medication Name
Dosage	Dosage
Route (*by mouth, injected, etc.*)	Route (*by mouth, injected, etc.*)
Frequency (*how often taken*)	Frequency (*how often taken*)
Indication (*reason for taking*)	Indication (*reason for taking*)
Prescribing Doctor	Prescribing Doctor

Medication Name	Medication Name
Dosage	Dosage
Route (*by mouth, injected, etc.*)	Route (*by mouth, injected, etc.*)
Frequency (*how often taken*)	Frequency (*how often taken*)
Indication (*reason for taking*)	Indication (*reason for taking*)
Prescribing Doctor	Prescribing Doctor

Medication Name	Medication Name
Dosage	Dosage
Route (*by mouth, injected, etc.*)	Route (*by mouth, injected, etc.*)
Frequency (*how often taken*)	Frequency (*how often taken*)
Indication (*reason for taking*)	Indication (*reason for taking*)
Prescribing Doctor	Prescribing Doctor

Additional Information & Updates: (Please be as specific as possible and date all changes.)

_____
_____
_____
_____
_____
_____
_____
_____
_____
_____

If you have received Durable Medical Equipment (DME) supplies or any assistive devices, be sure to itemize them below. _(Wheelchairs, hospital beds, walkers, oxygen, hearing aids, etc.)_

ASSISTIVE DEVICE	PRESCRIBING DOCTOR	DME SUPPLY COMPANY	PHONE #

Additional Information & Updates: (Please be as specific as possible and date all changes.)

_____
_____
_____
_____
_____
_____
_____
_____
_____

PEDIATRICIAN

PEDIATRICIAN	
Doctor's Name	
Doctor's Office Phone #	
Doctor's Cell Phone #	
Doctor's Office Fax #	
Emergency Hotline #	
Doctor's Office Email Address	
Doctor's Office Website	
Patient Portal Login	
Patient Portal Password	
Patient Portal Pin #	
Doctor's Office Address	
City	
State	
Zip Code	
Billing Phone #	
Billing Address	
City	
State	
Zip Code	

Additional Information & Updates: (Please be as specific as possible and date all changes.)

_____

_____

_____

_____

_____

_____

_____

_____

_____

MEDICAL SPECIALISTS

Check below to indicate what types of medical **specialists** your child utilizes, if any. Provide contact information for any specialist checked below.

☐ **Audiologist** ☐ Phone #	☐ **Infectious Disease** ☐ Phone #	☐ **Ophthalmologist** ☐ Phone #	☐ **Psychiatrist** ☐ Phone #
☐ **Cardiologist** ☐ Phone #	☐ **Mental Health** ☐ Phone #	☐ **Optician** ☐ Phone #	☐ **Psychotherapist** ☐ Phone #
☐ **Dentist** ☐ Phone #	☐ **Neonatologist** ☐ Phone #	☐ **Orthodontist** ☐ Phone #	☐ **Pulmonologist** ☐ Phone #
☐ **Dermatologist** ☐ Phone #	☐ **Nephrologist** ☐ Phone #	☐ **Orthopedic** ☐ Phone #	☐ **Rheumatologist** ☐ Phone #
☐ **Endocrinologist** ☐ Phone #	☐ **Neurologist** ☐ Phone #	☐ **Otolaryngologist (ENT)** ☐ Phone #	☐ **Speech Therapist** ☐ Phone #
☐ **Gastroenterologist** ☐ Phone #	☐ **Nutritionist** ☐ Phone #	☐ **Pathologist** ☐ Phone #	☐ **Substance Abuse** ☐ Phone #
☐ **General Surgeon** ☐ Phone #	☐ **OBGYN** ☐ Phone #	☐ **Physical Therapist** ☐ Phone #	☐ **Urologist** ☐ Phone #
☐ **Hematologist** ☐ Phone #	☐ **Occupational Therapist** ☐ Phone #	☐ **Plastic Surgeon** ☐ Phone #	☐ **Other:** ☐ Phone #
☐ **Immunologist** ☐ Phone #	☐ **Oncologist** ☐ Phone #	☐ **Podiatrist** ☐ Phone #	☐ **Other:** ☐ Phone #

Additional Information, Physician Contact Information & Updates: (Please be as specific as possible and date all changes.)

_____

_____

_____

_____

_____

_____

_____

_____

_____

CHILD(REN)'S HEALTH & MEDICAL PROFILE (#4)

Child's Full Name: _____

Date of Birth: _____

HEALTH ALERTS

HEALTH ALERTS	
Blood Type	
Medication Allergies	
Food Allergies	
Other	

Additional Information & Updates: (Please be as specific as possible and date all changes.)

_____

_____

_____

_____

_____

_____

_____

_____

_____

_____

DIAGNOSIS

Diagnosis		Diagnosis	
Year Diagnosed		Year Diagnosed	
Doctor		Doctor	
Surgery	Yes / No	Surgery	Yes / No
If yes, Date of Surgery		If yes, Date of Surgery	
Final Report Attached	Yes / No	Final Report Attached	Yes / No

Diagnosis		Diagnosis	
Year Diagnosed		Year Diagnosed	
Doctor		Doctor	
Surgery	Yes / No	Surgery	Yes / No
If yes, Date of Surgery		If yes, Date of Surgery	
Final Report Attached	Yes / No	Final Report Attached	Yes / No

Additional Information & Updates: (Please be as specific as possible and date all changes.)

_____
_____
_____
_____
_____
_____
_____
_____
_____

MEDICATIONS

PHARMACY NAME	PHONE #

Medication Name	Medication Name
Dosage	Dosage
Route (*by mouth, injected, etc.*)	Route (*by mouth, injected, etc.*)
Frequency (*how often taken*)	Frequency (*how often taken*)
Indication (*reason for taking*)	Indication (*reason for taking*)
Prescribing Doctor	Prescribing Doctor

Medication Name	Medication Name
Dosage	Dosage
Route (*by mouth, injected, etc.*)	Route (*by mouth, injected, etc.*)
Frequency (*how often taken*)	Frequency (*how often taken*)
Indication (*reason for taking*)	Indication (*reason for taking*)
Prescribing Doctor	Prescribing Doctor

Medication Name	Medication Name
Dosage	Dosage
Route (*by mouth, injected, etc.*)	Route (*by mouth, injected, etc.*)
Frequency (*how often taken*)	Frequency (*how often taken*)
Indication (*reason for taking*)	Indication (*reason for taking*)
Prescribing Doctor	Prescribing Doctor

Additional Information & Updates: (Please be as specific as possible and date all changes.)

_____
_____
_____
_____
_____
_____
_____
_____

If you have received Durable Medical Equipment (DME) supplies or any assistive devices, be sure to itemize them below. _(Wheelchairs, hospital beds, walkers, oxygen, hearing aids, etc.)_

ASSISTIVE DEVICE	PRESCRIBING DOCTOR	DME SUPPLY COMPANY	PHONE #

Additional Information & Updates: (Please be as specific as possible and date all changes.)

_____
_____
_____
_____
_____
_____
_____
_____
_____

PEDIATRICIAN

PEDIATRICIAN	
Doctor's Name	
Doctor's Office Phone #	
Doctor's Cell Phone #	
Doctor's Office Fax #	
Emergency Hotline #	
Doctor's Office Email Address	
Doctor's Office Website	
Patient Portal Login	
Patient Portal Password	
Patient Portal Pin #	
Doctor's Office Address	
City	
State	
Zip Code	
Billing Phone #	
Billing Address	
City	
State	
Zip Code	

Additional Information & Updates: (Please be as specific as possible and date all changes.)

_____

_____

_____

_____

_____

_____

_____

_____

_____

MEDICAL SPECIALISTS

Check below to indicate what types of medical **specialists** your child utilizes, if any. Provide contact information for any specialist checked below.

☐ **Audiologist**	☐ **Infectious Disease**	☐ **Ophthalmologist**	☐ **Psychiatrist**
☐ Phone #	☐ Phone #	☐ Phone #	☐ Phone #
☐ **Cardiologist**	☐ **Mental Health**	☐ **Optician**	☐ **Psychotherapist**
☐ Phone #	☐ Phone #	☐ Phone #	☐ Phone #
☐ **Dentist**	☐ **Neonatologist**	☐ **Orthodontist**	☐ **Pulmonologist**
☐ Phone #	☐ Phone #	☐ Phone #	☐ Phone #
☐ **Dermatologist**	☐ **Nephrologist**	☐ **Orthopedic**	☐ **Rheumatologist**
☐ Phone #	☐ Phone #	☐ Phone #	☐ Phone #
☐ **Endocrinologist**	☐ **Neurologist**	☐ **Otolaryngologist (ENT)**	☐ **Speech Therapist**
☐ Phone #	☐ Phone #	☐ Phone #	☐ Phone #
☐ **Gastroenterologist**	☐ **Nutritionist**	☐ **Pathologist**	☐ **Substance Abuse**
☐ Phone #	☐ Phone #	☐ Phone #	☐ Phone #
☐ **General Surgeon**	☐ **OBGYN**	☐ **Physical Therapist**	☐ **Urologist**
☐ Phone #	☐ Phone #	☐ Phone #	☐ Phone #
☐ **Hematologist**	☐ **Occupational Therapist**	☐ **Plastic Surgeon**	☐ **Other:**
☐ Phone #	☐ Phone #	☐ Phone #	☐ Phone #
☐ **Immunologist**	☐ **Oncologist**	☐ **Podiatrist**	☐ **Other:**
☐ Phone #	☐ Phone #	☐ Phone #	☐ Phone #

Additional Information, Physician Contact Information & Updates: (Please be as specific as possible and date all changes.)

_____

_____

_____

_____

_____

_____

_____

_____

_____

CHILD(REN)'S HEALTH & MEDICAL PROFILE (#5)

Child's Full Name: _____

Date of Birth: _____

HEALTH ALERTS

HEALTH ALERTS	
Blood Type	
Medication Allergies	
Food Allergies	
Other	

Additional Information & Updates: (Please be as specific as possible and date all changes.)

_____

_____

_____

_____

_____

_____

_____

_____

DIAGNOSIS

Diagnosis	
Year Diagnosed	
Doctor	
Surgery	Yes / No
If yes, Date of Surgery	
Final Report Attached	Yes / No

Diagnosis	
Year Diagnosed	
Doctor	
Surgery	Yes / No
If yes, Date of Surgery	
Final Report Attached	Yes / No

Diagnosis	
Year Diagnosed	
Doctor	
Surgery	Yes / No
If yes, Date of Surgery	
Final Report Attached	Yes / No

Diagnosis	
Year Diagnosed	
Doctor	
Surgery	Yes / No
If yes, Date of Surgery	
Final Report Attached	Yes / No

Additional Information & Updates: (Please be as specific as possible and date all changes.)

_____

_____

_____

_____

_____

_____

_____

_____

_____

MEDICATIONS

PHARMACY NAME	PHONE #

Medication Name	Medication Name
Dosage	Dosage
Route (*by mouth, injected, etc.*)	Route (*by mouth, injected, etc.*)
Frequency (*how often taken*)	Frequency (*how often taken*)
Indication (*reason for taking*)	Indication (*reason for taking*)
Prescribing Doctor	Prescribing Doctor

Medication Name	Medication Name
Dosage	Dosage
Route (*by mouth, injected, etc.*)	Route (*by mouth, injected, etc.*)
Frequency (*how often taken*)	Frequency (*how often taken*)
Indication (*reason for taking*)	Indication (*reason for taking*)
Prescribing Doctor	Prescribing Doctor

Medication Name	Medication Name
Dosage	Dosage
Route (*by mouth, injected, etc.*)	Route (*by mouth, injected, etc.*)
Frequency (*how often taken*)	Frequency (*how often taken*)
Indication (*reason for taking*)	Indication (*reason for taking*)
Prescribing Doctor	Prescribing Doctor

Additional Information & Updates: (Please be as specific as possible and date all changes.)

If you have received Durable Medical Equipment (DME) supplies or any assistive devices, be sure to itemize them below. *(Wheelchairs, hospital beds, walkers, oxygen, hearing aids, etc.)*

ASSISTIVE DEVICE	PRESCRIBING DOCTOR	DME SUPPLY COMPANY	PHONE #

Additional Information & Updates: (Please be as specific as possible and date all changes.)

PEDIATRICIAN

PEDIATRICIAN	
Doctor's Name	
Doctor's Office Phone #	
Doctor's Cell Phone #	
Doctor's Office Fax #	
Emergency Hotline #	
Doctor's Office Email Address	
Doctor's Office Website	
Patient Portal Login	
Patient Portal Password	
Patient Portal Pin #	
Doctor's Office Address	
City	
State	
Zip Code	
Billing Phone #	
Billing Address	
City	
State	
Zip Code	

Additional Information & Updates: (Please be as specific as possible and date all changes.)

_____

_____

_____

_____

_____

_____

_____

_____

_____

MEDICAL SPECIALISTS

Check below to indicate what types of medical **specialists** your child utilizes, if any. Provide contact information for any specialist checked below.

☐ **Audiologist** ☐ Phone #	☐ **Infectious Disease** ☐ Phone #	☐ **Ophthalmologist** ☐ Phone #	☐ **Psychiatrist** ☐ Phone #
☐ **Cardiologist** ☐ Phone #	☐ **Mental Health** ☐ Phone #	☐ **Optician** ☐ Phone #	☐ **Psychotherapist** ☐ Phone #
☐ **Dentist** ☐ Phone #	☐ **Neonatologist** ☐ Phone #	☐ **Orthodontist** ☐ Phone #	☐ **Pulmonologist** ☐ Phone #
☐ **Dermatologist** ☐ Phone #	☐ **Nephrologist** ☐ Phone #	☐ **Orthopedic** ☐ Phone #	☐ **Rheumatologist** ☐ Phone #
☐ **Endocrinologist** ☐ Phone #	☐ **Neurologist** ☐ Phone #	☐ **Otolaryngologist (ENT)** ☐ Phone #	☐ **Speech Therapist** ☐ Phone #
☐ **Gastroenterologist** ☐ Phone #	☐ **Nutritionist** ☐ Phone #	☐ **Pathologist** ☐ Phone #	☐ **Substance Abuse** ☐ Phone #
☐ **General Surgeon** ☐ Phone #	☐ **OBGYN** ☐ Phone #	☐ **Physical Therapist** ☐ Phone #	☐ **Urologist** ☐ Phone #
☐ **Hematologist** ☐ Phone #	☐ **Occupational Therapist** ☐ Phone #	☐ **Plastic Surgeon** ☐ Phone #	☐ **Other:** ☐ Phone #
☐ **Immunologist** ☐ Phone #	☐ **Oncologist** ☐ Phone #	☐ **Podiatrist** ☐ Phone #	☐ **Other:** ☐ Phone #

Additional Information, Physician Contact Information & Updates: (Please be as specific as possible and date all changes.)

_____

_____

_____

_____

_____

_____

_____

_____

_____

CHILD(REN)'S HEALTH & MEDICAL PROFILE (#6)

Child's Full Name: _____

Date of Birth: _____

HEALTH ALERTS

HEALTH ALERTS	
Blood Type	
Medication Allergies	
Food Allergies	
Other	

Additional Information & Updates: (Please be as specific as possible and date all changes.)

_____

_____

_____

_____

_____

_____

_____

_____

_____

_____

DIAGNOSIS

Diagnosis		Diagnosis	
Year Diagnosed		Year Diagnosed	
Doctor		Doctor	
Surgery	Yes / No	Surgery	Yes / No
If yes, Date of Surgery		If yes, Date of Surgery	
Final Report Attached	Yes / No	Final Report Attached	Yes / No

Diagnosis		Diagnosis	
Year Diagnosed		Year Diagnosed	
Doctor		Doctor	
Surgery	Yes / No	Surgery	Yes / No
If yes, Date of Surgery		If yes, Date of Surgery	
Final Report Attached	Yes / No	Final Report Attached	Yes / No

Additional Information & Updates: (Please be as specific as possible and date all changes.)

_____

_____

_____

_____

_____

_____

_____

_____

_____

MEDICATIONS

PHARMACY NAME	PHONE #

Medication Name	**Medication Name**
Dosage	Dosage
Route (*by mouth, injected, etc.*)	Route (*by mouth, injected, etc.*)
Frequency (*how often taken*)	Frequency (*how often taken*)
Indication (*reason for taking*)	Indication (*reason for taking*)
Prescribing Doctor	Prescribing Doctor

Medication Name	**Medication Name**
Dosage	Dosage
Route (*by mouth, injected, etc.*)	Route (*by mouth, injected, etc.*)
Frequency (*how often taken*)	Frequency (*how often taken*)
Indication (*reason for taking*)	Indication (*reason for taking*)
Prescribing Doctor	Prescribing Doctor

Medication Name	**Medication Name**
Dosage	Dosage
Route (*by mouth, injected, etc.*)	Route (*by mouth, injected, etc.*)
Frequency (*how often taken*)	Frequency (*how often taken*)
Indication (*reason for taking*)	Indication (*reason for taking*)
Prescribing Doctor	Prescribing Doctor

Additional Information & Updates: (Please be as specific as possible and date all changes.)

_____
_____
_____
_____
_____
_____
_____
_____
_____
_____

If you have received Durable Medical Equipment (DME) supplies or any assistive devices, be sure to itemize them below. *(Wheelchairs, hospital beds, walkers, oxygen, hearing aids, etc.)*

ASSISTIVE DEVICE	PRESCRIBING DOCTOR	DME SUPPLY COMPANY	PHONE #

Additional Information & Updates: (Please be as specific as possible and date all changes.)

_____
_____
_____
_____
_____
_____
_____
_____
_____
_____

PEDIATRICIAN

PEDIATRICIAN	
Doctor's Name	
Doctor's Office Phone #	
Doctor's Cell Phone #	
Doctor's Office Fax #	
Emergency Hotline #	
Doctor's Office Email Address	
Doctor's Office Website	
Patient Portal Login	
Patient Portal Password	
Patient Portal Pin #	
Doctor's Office Address	
City	
State	
Zip Code	
Billing Phone #	
Billing Address	
City	
State	
Zip Code	

Additional Information & Updates: (Please be as specific as possible and date all changes.)

_____

_____

_____

_____

_____

_____

_____

_____

_____

MEDICAL SPECIALISTS

Check below to indicate what types of medical **specialists** your child utilizes, if any. Provide contact information for any specialist checked below.

☐ **Audiologist** ☐ Phone #	☐ **Infectious Disease** ☐ Phone #	☐ **Ophthalmologist** ☐ Phone #	☐ **Psychiatrist** ☐ Phone #
☐ **Cardiologist** ☐ Phone #	☐ **Mental Health** ☐ Phone #	☐ **Optician** ☐ Phone #	☐ **Psychotherapist** ☐ Phone #
☐ **Dentist** ☐ Phone #	☐ **Neonatologist** ☐ Phone #	☐ **Orthodontist** ☐ Phone #	☐ **Pulmonologist** ☐ Phone #
☐ **Dermatologist** ☐ Phone #	☐ **Nephrologist** ☐ Phone #	☐ **Orthopedic** ☐ Phone #	☐ **Rheumatologist** ☐ Phone #
☐ **Endocrinologist** ☐ Phone #	☐ **Neurologist** ☐ Phone #	☐ **Otolaryngologist (ENT)** ☐ Phone #	☐ **Speech Therapist** ☐ Phone #
☐ **Gastroenterologist** ☐ Phone #	☐ **Nutritionist** ☐ Phone #	☐ **Pathologist** ☐ Phone #	☐ **Substance Abuse** ☐ Phone #
☐ **General Surgeon** ☐ Phone #	☐ **OBGYN** ☐ Phone #	☐ **Physical Therapist** ☐ Phone #	☐ **Urologist** ☐ Phone #
☐ **Hematologist** ☐ Phone #	☐ **Occupational Therapist** ☐ Phone #	☐ **Plastic Surgeon** ☐ Phone #	☐ **Other:** ☐ Phone #
☐ **Immunologist** ☐ Phone #	☐ **Oncologist** ☐ Phone #	☐ **Podiatrist** ☐ Phone #	☐ **Other:** ☐ Phone #

Additional Information, Physician Contact Information & Updates: (Please be as specific as possible and date all changes.)

_____

_____

_____

_____

_____

_____

_____

_____

4.4 PERSONS WITH DISABILITIES OR SPECIAL NEEDS

Child's Full Name: _____

Date of Birth: _____

EDUCATION

School Name	
School Phone #	
IEP Team Evaluator's Name	
IEP Team Evaluator's Phone #	
Teacher's Name	
Teacher's Phone #	
Special Education Teacher's Name	
Special Education Teacher's Phone #	
ABA Provider	
ABA Provider Phone #	
School Social Worker's Name	
Social Worker's Phone #	
School Nurse's Name	
Nurse's Phone #	

Additional Information & Updates: (Please be as specific as possible and date all changes.)

_____
_____
_____
_____
_____
_____
_____
_____
_____
_____

TRANSPORTATION

Transportation Company Name	
Transportation Phone #	
Dispatcher's Name	
Dispatcher's Cell Phone #	
Driver's Name	
Driver's Cell Phone #	
Days of Transport (*Circle one*)	M / Tu / W / Th / Fri / Sat / Sun
Pick Up Time	
Pick Up Address	
City, State & Zip Code	
Drop Off Time	
Drop Off Address	
City, State & Zip Code	

Additional Information & Updates: (Please be as specific as possible and date all changes.)

_____

_____

_____

_____

_____

_____

_____

_____

_____

_____

PHYSICAL THERAPY

Physical Therapy Group Name	
Group Phone #	
Physical Therapist Name	
Physical Therapist Cell Phone #	
Days of Attendance	M / Tu / W / Th / Fri / Sat / Sun
Hours of Attendance	
Treatment Plan	Attach as Directed

Additional Information & Updates: (Please be as specific as possible and date all changes.)

_____
_____
_____
_____
_____
_____
_____
_____
_____

OCCUPATIONAL THERAPY

Occupational Therapy Group Name	
Group Phone #	
Occupational Therapist Name	
Occupational Therapist Cell Phone #	
Days of Attendance	M / Tu / W / Th / Fri / Sat / Sun
Hours of Attendance	
Treatment Plan	Attach as Directed

Additional Information & Updates: (Please be as specific as possible and date all changes.)

_____
_____
_____
_____
_____
_____
_____
_____
_____

SPEECH THERAPY

Speech Therapy Group Name	
Group Phone #	

Speech Therapist Name	
Speech Therapist Cell Phone #	
Days of Attendance	M / Tu / W / Th / Fri / Sat / Sun
Hours of Attendance	
Treatment Plan	Attach as Directed

Additional Information & Updates: (Please be as specific as possible and date all changes.)

_____
_____
_____
_____
_____
_____
_____
_____
_____
_____

BEHAVIORAL THERAPY

Behavioral Therapy Group Name	
Group Phone #	
Behavioral Specialist Name	
Behavioral Specialist Cell Phone #	
Days of Attendance	M / Tu / W / Th / Fri / Sat / Sun
Hours of Attendance	
Treatment Plan	Attach as Directed

Additional Information & Updates: (Please be as specific as possible and date all changes.)

_____
_____
_____
_____
_____
_____
_____
_____

If you have received Durable Medical Equipment (DME) supplies or any assistive devices, be sure to itemize them below. *(Wheelchairs, hospital beds, walkers, oxygen, hearing aids, etc.)*

ASSISTIVE DEVICE	PRESCRIBING DOCTOR	DME SUPPLY COMPANY	PHONE #

Additional Information & Updates: (Please be as specific as possible and date all changes.)

4.5 CHILD(REN)'S FINANCIAL PROFILE

CHILD(REN)'S BANKING

PRIMARY BANK ACCOUNT	CHILD'S NAME:	CHILD'S NAME:
Family Member Name		
Bank Name		
Account Holder Name		
Joint Account (*Circle one*)	Yes / No	Yes / No
Joint Account Member Name		
Member ID/Access #		
Account Type	Savings	Savings
Account #		
Routing #		
Account Type	Checking	Checking
Account #		
Routing #		
Debit Card Account #		
Debit Card Pin #		
Debit Card CVV #		
Toll-Free Banking Phone #		
Local Branch Person of Contact		
Local Branch Phone #	Ext.	Ext.
Local Branch Fax #		
Person of Contact Email Address		
Bank Website		
Banking Login		
Banking Password		
Banking Pin #		
Security Word/Code		
Security Questions & Answers		
2-Step Verification Enabled	Yes / No	Yes / No
2-Step Verification (*Circle one*)	Email / Cell Phone #	Email / Cell Phone #
2-Step Verification Email		
2-Step Verification Email Password		

2-Step Verification Cell Phone #		
Local Branch Address		
City		
State		
Zip Code		

Additional Information & Updates: (Please be as specific as possible and date all changes.)

_____

_____

_____

_____

_____

_____

_____

_____

_____

_____

PRIMARY BANK ACCOUNT	CHILD'S NAME:	CHILD'S NAME:
Family Member Name		
Bank Name		
Account Holder Name		
Joint Account (Circle one)	Yes / No	Yes / No
Joint Account Member Name		
Member ID/Access #		
Account Type	Savings	Savings
Account #		
Routing #		
Account Type	Checking	Checking
Account #		
Routing #		
Debit Card Account #		
Debit Card Pin #		
Debit Card CVV #		
Toll-Free Banking Phone #		
Local Branch Person of Contact		
Local Branch Phone #	Ext.	Ext.
Local Branch Fax #		
Person of Contact Email Address		

Bank Website		
Banking Login		
Banking Password		
Banking Pin #		
Security Word/Code		
Security Questions & Answers		
2-Step Verification Enabled	Yes / No	Yes / No
2-Step Verification (*Circle one*)	Email / Cell Phone #	Email / Cell Phone #
2-Step Verification Email		
2-Step Verification Email Password		
2-Step Verification Cell Phone #		
Local Branch Address		
City		
State		
Zip Code		

Additional Information & Updates: (Please be as specific as possible and date all changes.)

_____
_____
_____
_____
_____
_____
_____
_____
_____
_____

PRIMARY BANK ACCOUNT	CHILD'S NAME:	CHILD'S NAME:
Family Member Name		
Bank Name		
Account Holder Name		
Joint Account (*Circle one*)	Yes / No	Yes / No
Joint Account Member Name		
Member ID/Access #		
Account Type	Savings	Savings

Account #		
Routing #		
Account Type	Checking	Checking
Account #		
Routing #		
Debit Card Account #		
Debit Card Pin #		
Debit Card CVV #		
Toll-Free Banking Phone #		
Local Branch Person of Contact		
Local Branch Phone #	Ext.	Ext.
Local Branch Fax #		
Person of Contact Email Address		
Bank Website		
Banking Login		
Banking Password		
Banking Pin #		
Security Word/Code		
Security Questions & Answers		
2-Step Verification Enabled	Yes / No	Yes / No
2-Step Verification (Circle one)	Email / Cell Phone #	Email / Cell Phone #
2-Step Verification Email		
2-Step Verification Email Password		
2-Step Verification Cell Phone #		
Local Branch Address		
City		
State		
Zip Code		

Additional Information & Updates: (Please be as specific as possible and date all changes.)

_____

_____

_____

_____

_____

STUDENT LOAN

STUDENT LOAN	STUDENT NAME:	STUDENT NAME:
Family Member Name		
Bank Name		
Account Holder Name		
Joint Account (*Circle one*)	Yes / No	Yes / No
Joint Account Member Name		
Member ID/Access #		
Loan Type		
Account #		
Amount Borrowed	$	$
Security Word/Code		
Toll-Free Banking Phone #		
Bank Website		
Banking Login		
Banking Login Password		
2-Step Verification Enabled	Yes / No	Yes / No
2-Step Verification (*Circle one*)	Email / Cell Phone #	Email / Cell Phone #
2-Step Verification Email		
2-Step Verification Email Password		
2-Step Verification Cell Phone #		
Local Branch Address		
City		
State		
Zip Code		

Additional Information & Updates: (Please be as specific as possible and date all changes.)

_____

_____

_____

_____

_____

STUDENT LOAN	STUDENT NAME:	STUDENT NAME:
Family Member Name		
Bank Name		
Account Holder Name		
Joint Account (*Circle one*)	Yes / No	Yes / No
Joint Account Member Name		
Member ID/Access #		
Loan Type		
Account #		
Amount Borrowed	$	$
Security Word/Code		
Toll-Free Banking Phone #		
Bank Website		
Banking Login		
Banking Login Password		
2-Step Verification Enabled	Yes / No	Yes / No
2-Step Verification (*Circle one*)	Email / Cell Phone #	Email / Cell Phone #
2-Step Verification Email		
2-Step Verification Email Password		
2-Step Verification Cell Phone #		
Local Branch Address		
City		
State		
Zip Code		

Additional Information & Updates: (Please be as specific as possible and date all changes.)

_____

_____

_____

_____

_____

_____

STUDENT LOAN	STUDENT NAME:	STUDENT NAME:
Family Member Name		
Bank Name		
Account Holder Name		
Joint Account (*Circle one*)	Yes / No	Yes / No
Joint Account Member Name		
Member ID/Access #		
Loan Type		
Account #		
Amount Borrowed	$	$
Security Word/Code		
Toll-Free Banking Phone #		
Bank Website		
Banking Login		
Banking Login Password		
2-Step Verification Enabled	Yes / No	Yes / No
2-Step Verification (*Circle one*)	Email / Cell Phone #	Email / Cell Phone #
2-Step Verification Email		
2-Step Verification Email Password		
2-Step Verification Cell Phone #		
Local Branch Address		
City		
State		
Zip Code		

Additional Information & Updates: (Please be as specific as possible and date all changes.)

INVESTMENTS

INVESTMENT FUND	CHILD'S NAME:	CHILD'S NAME:
Family Member Name		
Company Name		
Company Phone #		
Type of Fund		
Annual % Contribution		
Employer % Contribution		
Policy/Contract #		
Person of Contact Name		
Office Phone #		
Office Fax #		
Email Address		
Beneficiary Name		
Beneficiary Phone #		
Beneficiary Cell Phone #		
Beneficiary Email Address		
Beneficiary Address		
City		
State		
Zip Code		
Website		
Fund Login		
Fund Password		
Fund Pin #		
Security Password/Code		
2-Step Verification Enabled	Yes / No	Yes / No
2-Step Verification (*Circle one*)	Email / Cell Phone #	Email / Cell Phone #
2-Step Verification Email		
2-Step Verification Email Password		
2-Step Verification Cell Phone #		
Company Address		
City		
State		
Zip Code		

Additional Information & Updates: (Please be as specific as possible and date all changes.)

_____
_____
_____
_____
_____
_____
_____
_____
_____

INVESTMENT FUND	CHILD'S NAME:	CHILD'S NAME:
Family Member Name		
Company Name		
Company Phone #		
Type of Fund		
Annual % Contribution		
Employer % Contribution		
Policy/Contract #		
Person of Contact Name		
Office Phone #		
Office Fax #		
Email Address		
Beneficiary Name		
Beneficiary Phone #		
Beneficiary Cell Phone #		
Beneficiary Email Address		
Beneficiary Address		
City		
State		
Zip Code		
Website		
Fund Login		
Fund Password		
Fund Pin #		
Security Password/Code		
2-Step Verification Enabled	Yes / No	Yes / No
2-Step Verification (_Circle one_)	Email / Cell Phone #	Email / Cell Phone #

2-Step Verification Email		
2-Step Verification Email Password		
2-Step Verification Cell Phone #		
Company Address		
City		
State		
Zip Code		

Additional Information & Updates: (Please be as specific as possible and date all changes.)

_____

_____

_____

_____

_____

_____

_____

_____

_____

_____

INVESTMENT FUND	CHILD'S NAME:	CHILD'S NAME:
Family Member Name		
Company Name		
Company Phone #		
Type of Fund		
Annual % Contribution		
Employer % Contribution		
Policy/Contract #		
Person of Contact Name		
Office Phone #		
Office Fax #		
Email Address		
Beneficiary Name		
Beneficiary Phone #		
Beneficiary Cell Phone #		
Beneficiary Email Address		
Beneficiary Address		
City		

State		
Zip Code		
Website		
Fund Login		
Fund Password		
Fund Pin #		
Security Password/Code		
2-Step Verification Enabled	Yes / No	Yes / No
2-Step Verification (*Circle one*)	Email / Cell Phone #	Email / Cell Phone #
2-Step Verification Email		
2-Step Verification Email Password		
2-Step Verification Cell Phone #		
Company Address		
City		
State		
Zip Code		

Additional Information & Updates: (Please be as specific as possible and date all changes.)

_____

_____

_____

_____

_____

_____

_____

_____

_____

CHILDREN & DEPENDENTS DOCUMENT CHECKLIST

Include a copy or originals of the following documents with your *Life Management Portfolio: A How-To-Guide for Organizing Your Life.*

Child(ren)'s Profile:

☐ Legal guardianship *(if applicable)*

☐ Last updated will

☐ Trust fund *(if applicable)*

☐ Baptismal/Christening Certificates

☐ Each child's school identification card (front and back)

☐ Calendar of extracurricular activities with days and times of attendance

☐ Template of each child's daily scheduled routine, especially for infants and toddlers

☐ Family safe word created and discussed

Child(ren)'s Health & Medical Profile:

☐ Health & Medical reports *(if applicable)*

☐ Medical Specialist contact information *(if applicable)*

☐ Persons with Disabilities & Special Needs – Provide or attach additional information (as needed)

☐ Durable Medical Equipment (DME) supplies list

☐ Mental Health Treatment contact information *(if applicable)*

☐ Substance Abuse Treatment contact information *(if applicable)*

Child(ren)'s Financial Profile:

☐ Recent bank statements (for all children & dependents)

☐ Recent student loan statements (for all children & dependents)

☐ Recent investment statements (for all children & dependents)

☐ Free Application for Federal Student Aid (FAFSA) form (for college students)

Notes - Explanation for items left unchecked:

_____
_____
_____
_____
_____
_____
_____
_____
_____

5.
FINANCIAL PROFILE

Money can be an uncomfortable topic in some families, and the challenge of coming clean about finances or trusting someone else with access to your money has even been the cause of some divorces. Working through this section will require an in-depth and honest look at your financial landscape—think of it as one more step you are taking to ensure your family is provided for, should life changes occur in the future. Where you keep your money and how you've chosen to invest it matters to your family in the case you are ever unable to provide for them directly.

The following sections will prompt you to review your accounts, investments, insurance plans and more, and while it is not meant to be a roadmap for long-term financial planning, some sections may prompt you to consider financial options you have not yet considered. So take this opportunity to stay abreast of your own finances, plan ahead for your loved ones, and involve them in the conversation to raise awareness.

➤ *In this section, you will gather information regarding the following areas:*

PERSONAL BANKING – It's not uncommon these days to have multiple bank accounts and credit cards, and while the bulk of your investments may not be in these accounts, your household's daily expenses are likely still paid through these avenues. Therefore, a roadmap to the various financial institutions you use will be necessary for anyone needing to navigate your finances.

LOANS – Loans can be financed cars, home equity lines of credit, or some extra cash, and can be taken out independently or jointly with your spouse/partner. Whatever the case, someone will be responsible for meeting your financial obligations even if you are unable to, so document it all here.

INVESTMENT FUNDS – Whether you have a diverse financial portfolio or your investments are held in one account, spend some time studying your statements as you map out this section. It may have been a while since you last evaluated these accounts, so take this time to get a clear understanding of your personal finances, and also review any settings such as paperless statements or automatic re-investing options.

RETIREMENT/PENSION FUNDS – Staying informed and in close contact with the employer or advisor who manages your retirement/pension fund(s) is important. Job changes present options to carry over your accounts, roll them over into new ones, or keep them where they are. Keeping your family updated on any changes to these funds is essential.

LIFE INSURANCE – Outside of a will, a life insurance policy is one of the most searched for documents after death. It can help families cover funeral expenses for the deceased, pay off mortgage accounts, or continue to meet financial obligations after the insured has passed on. A life insurance policy will be of no help to your family if it has been lost, you've hidden it away somewhere so secure no one can find it, or your family was never aware of it to begin with. There are stories of insurance companies failing to properly disburse funds, or changing ownership over time, leaving policies suspended in limbo over the transition. All this to say, don't think your life insurance policy is a done deal once you've purchased it. Do your due diligence as you complete this Portfolio: review your policy, check in with your designated beneficiaries, and confirm the company's information. Make every effort in reviewing your policy to ensure its accuracy, for the sake of those who may need it one day.

SAFE DEPOSIT BOX – Once considered the most secure location for important documents, jewelry and family heirlooms, your safe deposit box and how to access it can be vitally important for you and anyone needing to carry on your estate. A physical key is needed to access your safe deposit box, so leave clear instructions to it here.

HELPFUL TIPS

#1 If you use multiple financial institutions for personal banking, make note of each.

#2 Durable Power of Attorney for Finances is voided upon death.

#3 Joint accounts are an effective way to continue to have access to funds after a loved one passes on.

#4 Change your online banking passwords every six months, enable two-step verification, text notification and add a security passcode to keep your account secure at all times.

#5 Verify the status of insurance policies and educate yourself on any company disbursement policies and changes.

#6 If you do not have a will, now is a great time to explore your options. No matter how big or small your estate, a will is essential.

#7 Beware of designating minors as beneficiaries on policies. If a child is under 18 years of age, they may not be able to legally receive funds from life insurance policies.

#8 Obtain and review annual copies of your credit report to ensure its accuracy and to identify issues or discrepancies.

#9 Safe deposit box keys should be labeled and kept with your Life Management Portfolio: A How-To-Guide for Organizing Your Life.

#10 Be mindful of scams. Scammers target you online, through text messaging, emails and phone calls. Do not confirm or deny account information. Contact your financial institution directly yourself.

FINANCIAL PROFILE

PERSONAL BANKING

PRIMARY BANK ACCOUNT	FAMILY MEMBER #1	FAMILY MEMBER #2
Family Member Name		
Bank Name		
Account Holder Name		
Joint Account (*Circle one*)	Yes / No	Yes / No
Joint Account Member Name		
Member ID/Access #		
Account Type	Savings	Savings
Account #		
Routing #		
Account Type	Checking	Checking
Account #		
Routing #		
Debit Card Account #		
Debit Card Pin #		
Debit Card CVV #		
Toll-Free Banking Phone #		
Local Branch Person of Contact		
Local Branch Phone #	Ext.	Ext.
Local Branch Fax #		
Person of Contact Email Address		
Bank Website		
Banking Login		
Banking Password		
Banking Pin #		
Security Word/Code		
Security Questions & Answers		
2-Step Verification Enabled	Yes / No	Yes / No
2-Step Verification (*Circle one*)	Email / Cell Phone #	Email / Cell Phone #
2-Step Verification Email		
2-Step Verification Email Password		
2-Step Verification Cell Phone #		
Local Branch Address		

City		
State		
Zip Code		

Additional Information & Updates: (Please be as specific as possible and date all changes.)

_____

_____

_____

_____

_____

_____

_____

_____

_____

_____

SECONDARY BANK ACCOUNT	FAMILY MEMBER #1	FAMILY MEMBER #2
Family Member Name		
Bank Name		
Account Holder Name		
Joint Account (Circle one)	Yes / No	Yes / No
Joint Account Member Name		
Member ID/Access #		
Account Type	Savings	Savings
Account #		
Routing #		
Account Type	Checking	Checking
Account #		
Routing #		
Debit Card Account #		
Debit Card Pin #		
Debit Card CVV #		
Toll-Free Banking Phone #		
Local Branch Person of Contact		
Local Branch Phone #	Ext.	Ext.
Local Branch Fax #		
Person of Contact Email Address		
Bank Website		
Banking Login		

Banking Password		
Banking Pin #		
Security Word/Code		
Security Questions & Answers		
2-Step Verification Enabled	Yes / No	Yes / No
2-Step Verification (*Circle one*)	Email / Cell Phone #	Email / Cell Phone #
2-Step Verification Email		
2-Step Verification Email Password		
2-Step Verification Cell Phone #		
Local Branch Address		
City		
State		
Zip Code		

Additional Information & Updates: (Please be as specific as possible and date all changes.)

_____
_____
_____
_____
_____
_____
_____
_____
_____
_____

CREDIT CARDS

CREDIT CARDS	FAMILY MEMBER #1	FAMILY MEMBER #2
Family Member Name		
Bank Name		
Account Holder Name		
Joint Account (*Circle one*)	Yes / No	Yes / No
Joint Account Member Name		
Member ID/Access #		
Account Type		

Account #		
CVV #		
Toll-Free Banking Phone #		
Bank Website		
Banking Login		
Banking Login Password		
Security Word/Code		
Security Questions & Answers		
2-Step Verification Enabled	Yes / No	Yes / No
2-Step Verification (Circle one)	Email / Cell Phone #	Email / Cell Phone #
2-Step Verification Email		
2-Step Verification Email Password		
2-Step Verification Cell Phone #		
Local Branch Address		
City		
State		
Zip Code		

Additional Information & Updates: (Please be as specific as possible and date all changes.)

_____

_____

_____

_____

_____

_____

_____

_____

_____

CREDIT CARDS	FAMILY MEMBER #1	FAMILY MEMBER #2
Family Member Name		
Bank Name		
Account Holder Name		
Joint Account (Circle one)	Yes / No	Yes / No

Joint Account Member Name		
Member ID/Access #		
Account Type		
Account #		
CVV #		
Toll-Free Banking Phone #		
Bank Website		
Banking Login		
Banking Login Password		
Security Word/Code		
Security Questions & Answers		
2-Step Verification Enabled	Yes / No	Yes / No
2-Step Verification (*Circle one*)	Email / Cell Phone #	Email / Cell Phone #
2-Step Verification Email		
2-Step Verification Email Password		
2-Step Verification Cell Phone #		
Local Branch Address		
City		
State		
Zip Code		

Additional Information & Updates: (Please be as specific as possible and date all changes.)

_____
_____
_____
_____
_____
_____
_____
_____
_____
_____

LOANS

LOAN #1	FAMILY MEMBER #1	FAMILY MEMBER #2
Family Member Name		
Bank Name		
Account Holder Name		
Joint Account (Circle one)	Yes / No	Yes / No
Joint Account Member Name		
Member ID/Access #		
Loan Type		
Account #		
Amount Borrowed	$	$
Toll-Free Banking Phone #		
Bank Website		
Banking Login		
Banking Login Password		
Security Word/Code		
Security Questions & Answers		
2-Step Verification Enabled	Yes / No	Yes / No
2-Step Verification (Circle one)	Email / Cell Phone #	Email / Cell Phone #
2-Step Verification Email		
2-Step Verification Email Password		
2-Step Verification Cell Phone #		
Local Branch Address		
City		
State		
Zip Code		

Additional Information & Updates: (Please be as specific as possible and date all changes.)

_____

_____

_____

_____

_____

_____

_____

_____

_____

_____

LOAN #2	FAMILY MEMBER #1	FAMILY MEMBER #2
Family Member Name		
Bank Name		
Account Holder Name		
Joint Account (*Circle one*)	Yes / No	Yes / No
Joint Account Member Name		
Member ID/Access #		
Loan Type		
Account #		
Amount Borrowed	$	$
Toll-Free Banking Phone #		
Bank Website		
Banking Login		
Banking Login Password		
Security Word/Code		
Security Questions & Answers		
2-Step Verification Enabled	Yes / No	Yes / No
2-Step Verification (*Circle one*)	Email / Cell Phone #	Email / Cell Phone #
2-Step Verification Email		
2-Step Verification Email Password		
2-Step Verification Cell Phone #		
Local Branch Address		
City		
State		
Zip Code		

Additional Information & Updates: (Please be as specific as possible and date all changes.)

_____

_____

_____

_____

_____

_____

_____

_____

_____

_____

INVESTMENT FUND

INVESTMENT FUND #1	FAMILY MEMBER #1	FAMILY MEMBER #2
Family Member Name		
Company Name		
Company Phone #		
Type of Fund		
Annual % Contribution		
Employer % Contribution		
Policy/Contract #		
Person of Contact Name		
Office Phone #		
Office Fax #		
Email Address		
Beneficiary Name		
Beneficiary Phone #		
Beneficiary Cell Phone #		
Beneficiary Email Address		
Beneficiary Address		
City		
State		
Zip Code		
Website		
Fund Login		
Fund Password		
Fund Pin #		
Security Word/Code		
Security Questions & Answers		

2-Step Verification Enabled	Yes / No	Yes / No
2-Step Verification (*Circle one*)	Email / Cell Phone #	Email / Cell Phone #
2-Step Verification Email		
2-Step Verification Email Password		
2-Step Verification Cell Phone #		
Company Address		
City		
State		
Zip Code		

Additional Information & Updates: (Please be as specific as possible and date all changes.)

_____

_____

_____

_____

_____

_____

_____

_____

_____

_____

INVESTMENT FUND #2	FAMILY MEMBER #1	FAMILY MEMBER #2
Family Member Name		
Company Name		
Company Phone #		
Type of Fund		
Annual % Contribution		
Employer % Contribution		
Policy/Contract #		
Person of Contact Name		
Office Phone #		
Office Fax #		
Email Address		
Beneficiary Name		
Beneficiary Phone #		

Beneficiary Cell Phone #		
Beneficiary Email Address		
Beneficiary Address		
City		
State		
Zip Code		
Website		
Fund Login		
Fund Password		
Fund Pin #		
Security Word/Code		
Security Questions & Answers		
2-Step Verification Enabled	Yes / No	Yes / No
2-Step Verification (*Circle one*)	Email / Cell Phone #	Email / Cell Phone #
2-Step Verification Email		
2-Step Verification Email Password		
2-Step Verification Cell Phone #		
Company Address		
City		
State		
Zip Code		

Additional Information & Updates: (Please be as specific as possible and date all changes.)

_____
_____
_____
_____
_____
_____
_____
_____
_____

INVESTMENT FUND #3	FAMILY MEMBER #1	FAMILY MEMBER #2
Family Member Name		
Company Name		
Company Phone #		
Type of Fund		
Annual % Contribution		
Employer % Contribution		
Policy/Contract #		
Person of Contact Name		
Office Phone #		
Office Fax #		
Email Address		
Beneficiary Name		
Beneficiary Phone #		
Beneficiary Cell Phone #		
Beneficiary Email Address		
Beneficiary Address		
City		
State		
Zip Code		
Website		
Fund Login		
Fund Password		
Fund Pin #		
Security Word/Code		
Security Questions & Answers		
2-Step Verification Enabled	Yes / No	Yes / No
2-Step Verification (*Circle one*)	Email / Cell Phone #	Email / Cell Phone #
2-Step Verification Email		
2-Step Verification Email Password		
2-Step Verification Cell Phone #		
Company Address		
City		
State		
Zip Code		

Additional Information & Updates: (Please be as specific as possible and date all changes.)

_____

_____

_____

_____

_____

_____

_____

_____

_____

_____

RETIREMENT/PENSION

RETIREMENT/PENSION #1	FAMILY MEMBER #1	FAMILY MEMBER #2
Family Member Name		
Company Name		
Company Phone #		
Type of Fund		
Annual % Contribution		
Employer % Contribution		
Policy/Contract #		
Person of Contact Name		
Office Phone #		
Office Fax #		
Email Address		
Beneficiary Name		
Beneficiary Phone #		
Beneficiary Cell Phone #		
Beneficiary Email Address		
Beneficiary Address		
City		
State		
Zip Code		
Website		
Fund Login		
Fund Password		
Fund Pin #		

Security Word/Code		
Security Questions & Answers		
2-Step Verification Enabled	Yes / No	Yes / No
2-Step Verification (*Circle one*)	Email / Cell Phone #	Email / Cell Phone #
2-Step Verification Email		
2-Step Verification Email Password		
2-Step Verification Cell Phone #		
Company Address		
City		
State		
Zip Code		

Additional Information & Updates: (Please be as specific as possible and date all changes.)

_____
_____
_____
_____
_____
_____
_____
_____
_____
_____

RETIREMENT/PENSION #2	FAMILY MEMBER #1	FAMILY MEMBER #2
Family Member Name		
Company Name		
Company Phone #		
Type of Fund		
Annual % Contribution		
Employer % Contribution		
Policy/Contract #		
Person of Contact Name		
Office Phone #		
Office Fax #		

Email Address		
Beneficiary Name		
Beneficiary Phone #		
Beneficiary Cell Phone #		
Beneficiary Email Address		
Beneficiary Address		
City		
State		
Zip Code		
Website		
Fund Login		
Fund Password		
Fund Pin #		
Security Word/Code		
Security Questions & Answers		
2-Step Verification Enabled	Yes / No	Yes / No
2-Step Verification (*Circle one*)	Email / Cell Phone #	Email / Cell Phone #
2-Step Verification Email		
2-Step Verification Email Password		
2-Step Verification Cell Phone #		
Company Address		
City		
State		
Zip Code		

Additional Information & Updates: (Please be as specific as possible and date all changes.)

_____

_____

_____

_____

_____

_____

_____

_____

_____

LIFE INSURANCE

LIFE INSURANCE #1	FAMILY MEMBER #1	FAMILY MEMBER #2
Family Member Name		
Insured Member Name		
Insured Member DOB		
Company Name		
Company Phone #		
Type of Fund		
Monthly Payment Amount	$	$
Policy/Contract #		
Policy Effective Date		
Face Value Amount	$	$
Cash Surrender Value	$	$
Final Date of Policy		
Death Benefit Option	Yes / No	Yes / No
Death Benefit Amount	$	$
Agent Name		
Agent Office Phone #		
Agent Cell Phone #		
Agent Office Fax #		
Agent Email Address		
Beneficiary Name		
Beneficiary Phone #		
Beneficiary Cell Phone #		
Beneficiary Email Address		
Beneficiary Address		
City		
State		
Zip Code		
Website		
Fund Login		
Fund Password		
Fund Pin #		
Security Word/Code		
Security Questions & Answers		
2-Step Verification Enabled	Yes / No	Yes / No
2-Step Verification (*Circle one*)	Email / Cell Phone #	Email / Cell Phone #

2-Step Verification Email		
2-Step Verification Email Password		
2-Step Verification Cell Phone #		
Company Address		
City		
State		
Zip Code		

Additional Information & Updates: (Please be as specific as possible and date all changes.)

_____

_____

_____

_____

_____

_____

_____

_____

_____

_____

LIFE INSURANCE #2	FAMILY MEMBER #1	FAMILY MEMBER #2
Family Member Name		
Insured Member Name		
Insured Member DOB		
Company Name		
Company Phone #		
Type of Fund		
Monthly Payment Amount	$	$
Policy/Contract #		
Policy Effective Date		
Face Value Amount	$	$
Cash Surrender Value	$	$
Final Date of Policy		
Death Benefit Option	Yes / No	Yes / No
Death Benefit Amount	$	$
Agent Name		
Agent Office Phone #		
Agent Cell Phone #		
Agent Office Fax #		

Agent Email Address		
Beneficiary Name		
Beneficiary Phone #		
Beneficiary Cell Phone #		
Beneficiary Email Address		
Beneficiary Address		
City		
State		
Zip Code		
Website		
Fund Login		
Fund Password		
Fund Pin #		
Security Word/Code		
Security Questions & Answers		
2-Step Verification Enabled	Yes / No	Yes / No
2-Step Verification (*Circle one*)	Email / Cell Phone #	Email / Cell Phone #
2-Step Verification Email		
2-Step Verification Email Password		
2-Step Verification Cell Phone #		
Company Address		
City		
State		
Zip Code		

Additional Information & Updates: (Please be as specific as possible and date all changes.)

_____
_____
_____
_____
_____
_____
_____
_____
_____
_____

THE LIFE MANAGEMENT PORTFOLIO

SAFE DEPOSIT BOX

SAFE DEPOSIT BOX	FAMILY MEMBER #1	FAMILY MEMBER #2
Family Member Name		
Bank Name		
Account Holder Name		
Joint Account (*Circle one*)	Yes / No	Yes / No
Joint Account Member Name		
Member ID/Access #		
Account Type	Safe Deposit Box	Safe Deposit Box
Account #		
Key #		
Key Location		
Beneficiary Name		
Beneficiary Phone #		
Beneficiary Cell Phone #		
Beneficiary Email Address		
Beneficiary Address		
City		
State		
Zip Code		
Toll-Free Banking Phone #		
Local Branch Phone #	Ext.	Ext.
Local Branch Fax #		
Point of Contact Name		
Point of Contact Email Address		
Bank Website		
Deposit Box Location Address		
City		
State		
Zip Code		

Additional Information & Updates: (Please be as specific as possible and date all changes.)

_____

_____

_____

_____

_____

_____

_____

_____

_____

FINANCIAL PROFILE DOCUMENT CHECKLIST

Include a copy or originals of the following documents with your _Life Management Portfolio: A How-To-Guide for Organizing Your Life._

Personal/Secondary Banking:

☐ Recent primary and secondary banking statements

☐ Copies of debit cards (front and back)

Credit Cards:

☐ Recent credit card statement

☐ Copies of credit cards (front and back)

Loans:

☐ Loan statements – with terms and conditions of the loan

Investment Funds:

☐ Recent Investment funds statements – with terms and conditions of the fund

Retirement/Pension:

☐ Recent Retirement statements – with terms and conditions

☐ Recent Pension statements – with terms and conditions

Life Insurance:

☐ Life Insurance Policy – attach an original copy of your policies with your work-book

☐ Beneficiaries have been reviewed and updated on all enclosed policies

Safe Deposit Box:

☐ Safe deposit box – label and attach key to your portfolio

☐ Safe deposit box – itemized list of contents

Notes - Explanation for items left unchecked:

_____

_____

_____

_____

_____

_____

_____

_____

6.
REAL ESTATE PROFILE

Home ownership has long been a part of the American Dream. Many people work for years to buy their first home, and any property you own is likely to account for a sizable portion of your overall investment portfolio. Not to mention, your home is in many ways the base of everything else in your life. It's where you come back to at the end of the day, where you spend time with your loved ones, where your children feel safest and most comfortable, surrounded by familiarity and love.

Purchasing and owning a home is no simple matter – often involving mortgages, insurance, taxes, lawyers, and more. If your real estate portfolio includes properties that you own and run as rentals, you've probably added vendors, tenants, and more insurance policies to the mix. Completing this section of your *Life Management Portfolio: A How-To-Guide for Organizing Your Life* can help you stay on top of all these moving pieces, and help ensure that your loved ones will not lose their home in the event something unexpected should happen to the primary property owner. It will also help someone maintain your rental properties, ensuring that those holdings are properly managed and remain part of your portfolio.

➤ *In this section, you will gather information regarding the following areas:*

MORTGAGE BANKING – Whether you pay your mortgage consistently and on time greatly determines your credit score and financial reputation. It can also affect the viability of your home, leading to much stress for a family member who needs to know how to continue payment and with what funds. Noting this information here will help you and your family stay on top of mortgage payments.

HOMEOWNERS INSURANCE – These sorts of policies protect you in case of accidents, floods, weather, and injury, but many people pay their premiums automatically online, which doesn't always allow for an overview of the nuts and bolts of a policy. Make sure you know where to find your policy and take time to review it thoroughly.

PROPERTY TAXES – Like your mortgage, property taxes must be paid on time or you may be in danger of losing ownership of the property or land. This part of the workbook notes what to pay in taxes, when, and how, to keep your property in your hands.

REAL ESTATE LAWYER – If any legal professional played a role in assisting you in purchasing, refinancing or handling any legal affairs pertaining to your home, their information should be noted here.

NEW HOME CONSTRUCTION – Perhaps you chose the hands-on approach to home ownership. Having basic information on who to contact can be quite helpful if someone needs to assist or oversee the continued building of your dream home while you temporarily tend to other matters.

RENTAL PROPERTY – Just as tenants are responsible for paying their rent in a timely manner, property owners are entrusted with making sure tenants' needs are taken care of and the rental property is properly maintained. You might do this through a property manager, and likely with the help of certain vendors, whose information will be useful to note in case someone else must keep things running while you are away.

HELPFUL TIPS

#1 Your deed and title to your home proves ownership.

#2 Review the terms and conditions of your homeowners insurance policy yearly to be aware of any changes.

#3 Depending on your state, a homeowner's insurance policy may be canceled and non-transferable upon a sole homeowner's death.

#4 Unpaid property taxes may cause you to lose your home/land.

#5 Do yearly maintenance checks on your furnace and hot water tank for efficiency *(if applicable)*.

#6 Keep home warranties and service contracts in one location.

#7 Teach minor household members how to use the home alarm system *(if applicable)*.

REAL ESTATE PROFILE

MORTGAGE BANKING

MORTGAGE BANKING	PROPERTY #1	PROPERTY #2
Property Address		
City		
State		
Zip Code		
# of Acres		
Square footage of the home		
Used as rental property?	Yes / No	Yes / No
Bank Name		
Mortgage Holder Name		
Joint Account (*Circle one*)	Yes / No	Yes / No
Joint Account Member Name		
Member ID/Access #		
Account Type	Mortgage	Mortgage
Term of Mortgage		
Account #		
Monthly Payment Amount	$	$
Monthly Due Date		
Current Payoff Amount	$	$
Mortgage Free	Yes / No	Yes / No
(*If yes*) Is your property deed lien free?	Yes / No	Yes / No
Are your property taxes paid up-to-date?	Yes / No	Yes / No
(*If no*) Is there a current tax lien on the property?	Yes / No	Yes / No
Toll-Free Banking Phone #		
Local Branch Phone #	Ext.	Ext.
Local Branch Fax #		
Point of Contact Name		
Point of Contact Email Address		
Bank Website		
Banking Login		
Banking Password		

Banking Pin #		
Security Word/Code		
Security Questions & Answers		
2-Step Verification Enabled	Yes / No	Yes / No
2-Step Verification (Circle one)	Email / Cell Phone #	Email / Cell Phone #
2-Step Verification Email		
2-Step Verification Email Password		
2-Step Verification Cell Phone #		
Bank Address		
City		
State		
Zip Code		

Additional Information & Updates: (Please be as specific as possible and date all changes.)

_____

_____

_____

_____

_____

_____

_____

_____

_____

_____

HOMEOWNERS INSURANCE

HOMEOWNERS INSURANCE	PROPERTY #1	PROPERTY #2
Property Address		
City		
State		
Zip Code		
Homeowners Insurance Name		
Account Holder Name		
Joint Account (Circle one)	Yes / No	Yes / No
Joint Account Member Name		

Policy #		
Payment Amount	$ Mthly / Yearly	$ Mthly / Yearly
Due Date		
Do you forward the insurance declaration page to the bank?	Yes / No	Yes / No
(If yes) Name of Bank		
Bank Phone #		
Bank Fax #		
Bank Email Address		
Bank Address		
City		
State		
Zip Code		
Homeowners Insurance Website		
User Login		
User Password		
Pin #		
Security Word/Code		
2-Step Verification Enabled	Yes / No	Yes / No
2-Step Verification (*Circle one*)	Email / Cell Phone #	Email / Cell Phone #
2-Step Verification Email		
2-Step Verification Email Password		
2-Step Verification Cell Phone #		
Homeowners Insurance Address		
City		
State		
Zip Code		

Additional Information & Updates: (Please be as specific as possible and date all changes.)

_____

_____

_____

_____

_____

_____

_____

_____

_____

PROPERTY TAXES

PROPERTY TAXES	PROPERTY #1	PROPERTY #2
Receiver of Taxes		
Receiver of Taxes Phone #		
S.D. Code		
Section		
Block		
Lot		
Building		
Unit		
Receiver of Taxes Website		
Receiver of Taxes Address		
City		
State		
Zip Code		

Additional Information & Updates: (Please be as specific as possible and date all changes.)

_____

_____

_____

_____

_____

_____

_____

_____

_____

_____

REAL ESTATE LAWYER

REAL ESTATE LAWYER	PROPERTY #1	PROPERTY #2
Firm Name		
Lawyer Name		
Lawyer Office #		
Lawyer Cell Phone #		
Lawyer Email Address		

Firm Website		
Firm Address		
City		
State		
Zip Code		

Additional Information & Updates: (Please be as specific as possible and date all changes.)

_____

_____

_____

_____

_____

_____

_____

_____

_____

_____

NEW HOME CONSTRUCTION

NEW HOME CONSTRUCTION	PROPERTY #1	PROPERTY #2
Property Address		
City		
State		
Zip Code		
Builder's Company Name		
Office Phone #		
Builder's Agent Name		
Builder's Agent Cell Phone #		
Builder's Agent Email Address		
Buyer's Agent Name		
Buyer's Agent Cell Phone #		
Buyer's Agent Email Address		
Builder's Website		
Builder's Address		
City		
State		
Zip Code		

Additional Information & Updates: (Please be as specific as possible and date all changes.)

_____
_____
_____
_____
_____
_____
_____
_____
_____

MANAGEMENT OF RENTAL PROPERTY

MANAGEMENT OF RENTAL PROPERTY	RENTAL PROPERTY #1	RENTAL PROPERTY #2
Property Address		
City		
State		
Zip Code		
Receiver of Taxes		
Receiver of Taxes Phone #		
Management Company Name		
Management Office Phone #		
Management Agent Name		
Agent Cell Phone #		
Agent Email Address		
Management Company Website		
Management Address		
City		
State		
Zip Code		

Additional Information & Updates: (Please be as specific as possible and date all changes.)

_____
_____
_____

_____

_____

_____

_____

_____

_____

_____

MANAGEMENT OF RENTAL PROPERTY	RENTAL PROPERTY #3	RENTAL PROPERTY #4
Property Address		
City		
State		
Zip Code		
Receiver of Taxes		
Receiver of Taxes Phone #		
Management Company Name		
Management Office Phone #		
Management Agent Name		
Agent Cell Phone #		
Agent Email Address		
Management Company Website		
Management Address		
City		
State		
Zip Code		

Additional Information & Updates: (Please be as specific as possible and date all changes.)

_____

_____

_____

_____

_____

_____

_____

_____

RENTAL PROPERTY VENDORS

RENTAL PROPERTY VENDORS	RENTAL PROPERTY #1	RENTAL PROPERTY #1
Property Address		
City		
State		
Zip Code		
Utility Name		
Type of Service		
Account/Policy #		
Office Phone #		
Name on Account		
Email Address		
Website		
User Login		
User Password		
Pin #		
Security Word/Code		
Vendor Address		
City		
State		
Zip Code		

Additional Information & Updates: (Please be as specific as possible and date all changes.)

_____

_____

_____

_____

_____

_____

_____

_____

_____

RENTAL PROPERTY VENDORS	RENTAL PROPERTY #2	RENTAL PROPERTY #2
Property Address		
City		
State		
Zip Code		
Utility Name		
Type of Service		
Account/Policy #		
Office Phone #		
Name on Account		
Email Address		
Website		
User Login		
User Password		
Pin #		
Security Word/Code		
Vendor Address		
City		
State		
Zip Code		

Additional Information & Updates: (Please be as specific as possible and date all changes.)

_____
_____
_____
_____
_____
_____
_____
_____
_____
_____

RENTAL PROPERTY VENDORS	RENTAL PROPERTY #3	RENTAL PROPERTY #3
Property Address		
City		
State		
Zip Code		
Utility Name		
Type of Service		
Account/Policy #		
Office Phone #		
Name on Account		
Email Address		
Website		
User Login		
User Password		
Pin #		
Security Word/Code		
Vendor Address		
City		
State		
Zip Code		

Additional Information & Updates: (Please be as specific as possible and date all changes.)

_____

_____

_____

_____

_____

_____

_____

_____

_____

RENTAL PROPERTY VENDORS	RENTAL PROPERTY #4	RENTAL PROPERTY #5
Property Address		
City		
State		
Zip Code		
Utility Name		
Type of Service		
Account/Policy #		
Office Phone #		
Name on Account		
Email Address		
Website		
User Login		
User Password		
Pin #		
Security Word/Code		
Vendor Address		
City		
State		
Zip Code		

Additional Information & Updates: (Please be as specific as possible and date all changes.)

_____

_____

_____

_____

_____

_____

_____

_____

_____

REAL ESTATE DOCUMENT CHECKLIST

Include a copy or originals of the following documents with your *Life Management Portfolio: A How-To-Guide for Organizing Your Life.*

Property:

☐ Deed(s) on all properties

☐ Recent mortgage statement(s) for all properties *(if applicable)*

☐ Homeowners Insurance, with Declaration Page(s) for primary and rental property

☐ Recent Receiver of Taxes – Tax receipt/proof of payment status

☐ Maps of property lines *(if applicable)*

☐ Home alarm education and tutorial conducted for all household family members

New Home Constructions:

☐ New home construction contracts

☐ Land survey *(if applicable)*

☐ Permits for work done in or outside for property currently under construction

Rental Properties:

☐ Rental Property Management Agreement

☐ Rental agreement/tenant leases

☐ Renters' contact information

Notes - Explanation for items left unchecked:

_____
_____
_____
_____
_____
_____
_____
_____
_____
_____

7.
HOUSEHOLD EXPENSES

Take a moment and think back on what you had prioritized for today when you woke up this morning. Maybe you're helping your child with a school project, meeting a work deadline, or you're fresh out of groceries and need to run by the store. What you probably didn't think about was how to pay your electric bill, whether there will be water flowing from your sink, or if your Internet connection is working. A lot of the little things that go into running a home aren't things we are conscious of day-to-day, much less when there's a pressing emergency demanding all our attention.

These details of your household that take relatively little thought to maintain in regular times can present a big challenge to anyone needing to handle them on your behalf. Especially in the digital age of online accounts, autopay, and everything paperless, things are far more convenient but also far more obscure. This section of *The Life Management Portfolio: A How-To-Guide for Organizing Your Life* is a guide to help anyone who might need to take over little (but extremely important) things to keep your home up and running.

 In this section, you will gather information regarding the following areas:

HOME EXPENSES – Outlining utility companies in this section such as your electric, gas, heating, lighting, and cable providers at your primary place of residence, provide directions on how to maintain these services. If you have any streaming subscriptions such as Netflix, Hulu, Apple TV, Disney+, etc., it would be wise to include those as well. The information in this section lets multiple people share the responsibility of paying bills and managing accounts, on a regular basis or in times of emergency. It is especially useful to adult children residing out-of-state in assisting parents or grand-parents in navigating household expenses, if needed.

HELPFUL TIPS

#1 Some utility companies will not communicate with an individual unless they are designated on the account. Names can be added with permission, of course.

#2 Bills on autopay may not be so easily known. Take special care to note these accounts in your Portfolio.

#3 Paperless accounts leave no paper trail, making it all the more important to document their details.

HOME EXPENSES

HOME ADDRESS

HOME ADDRESS (PRIMARY RESIDENCE)	
Type of Residence (Circle One)	House / Condo / Apartment / Other:
Address	
City	
State	
Zip Code	

HOUSEHOLD VENDORS (PRIMARY RESIDENCE)

HOUSEHOLD VENDORS	VENDOR #1	VENDOR #2
Utility Company Name		
Type of Service		
Customer Service Phone #		
Account/Policy #		
Name on Account		
Joint Name on Account		
Phone # Associated with the Account	#	#
Amount Due (Approximate)	$	$
Due Date		
Billing Statement Received (Circle One)	Online / By Mail	Online / By Mail
Payment Made By (Circle One)	Online / Mail / Autopay / In-Person	Online / Mail / Autopay / In-Person
Utility Company Website		
User Login		
User Password		
Pin #		
Security Word/Code		
Company Address		
City		
State		
Zip Code		

Additional Information & Updates: (Please be as specific as possible and date all changes.)

_____

_____

_____

_____

_____

_____

_____

_____

_____

_____

HOUSEHOLD VENDORS	VENDOR #3	VENDOR #4
Utility Company Name		
Type of Service		
Customer Service Phone #		
Account/Policy #		
Name on Account		
Joint Name on Account		
Phone # Associated with the Account	#	#
Amount Due (*Approximate*)	$	$
Due Date		
Billing Statement Received (*Circle One*)	Online / By Mail	Online / By Mail
Payment Made By (*Circle One*)	Online / Mail / Autopay / In-Person	Online / Mail / Autopay / In-Person
Utility Company Website		
User Login		
User Password		
Pin #		
Security Word/Code		
Company Address		
City		
State		
Zip Code		

Additional Information & Updates: (Please be as specific as possible and date all changes.)

_____
_____
_____
_____
_____
_____
_____
_____
_____
_____

HOUSEHOLD VENDORS	VENDOR #5	VENDOR #6
Utility Company Name		
Type of Service		
Customer Service Phone #		
Account/Policy #		
Name on Account		
Joint Name on Account		
Phone # Associated with the Account	#	#
Amount Due (*Approximate*)	$	$
Due Date		
Billing Statement Received (*Circle One*)	Online / By Mail	Online / By Mail
Payment Made By (*Circle One*)	Online / Mail / Autopay / In-Person	Online / Mail / Autopay / In-Person
Utility Company Website		
User Login		
User Password		
Pin #		
Security Word/Code		
Company Address		
City		
State		
Zip Code		

Additional Information & Updates: (Please be as specific as possible and date all changes.)

_____

_____

_____

_____

_____

_____

_____

_____

_____

_____

HOUSEHOLD VENDORS	VENDOR #7	VENDOR #8
Utility Company Name		
Type of Service		
Customer Service Phone #		
Account/Policy #		
Name on Account		
Joint Name on Account		
Phone # Associated with the Account	#	#
Amount Due (_Approximate_)	$	$
Due Date		
Billing Statement Received (_Circle One_)	Online / By Mail	Online / By Mail
Payment Made By (_Circle One_)	Online / Mail / Autopay / In-Person	Online / Mail / Autopay / In-Person
Utility Company Website		
User Login		
User Password		
Pin #		
Security Word/Code		
Company Address		
City		
State		
Zip Code		

Additional Information & Updates: (Please be as specific as possible and date all changes.)

_____

_____

_____

_____

_____

_____

_____

_____

_____

_____

HOUSEHOLD VENDORS	VENDOR #9	VENDOR #10
Utility Company Name		
Type of Service		
Customer Service Phone #		
Account/Policy #		
Name on Account		
Joint Name on Account		
Phone # Associated with the Account	#	#
Amount Due (*Approximate*)	$	$
Due Date		
Billing Statement Received (*Circle One*)	Online / By Mail	Online / By Mail
Payment Made By (*Circle One*)	Online / Mail / Autopay / In-Person	Online / Mail / Autopay / In-Person
Utility Company Website		
User Login		
User Password		
Pin #		
Security Word/Code		
Company Address		
City		
State		
Zip Code		

Additional Information & Updates: (Please be as specific as possible and date all changes.)

_____
_____
_____
_____
_____
_____
_____
_____
_____

HOUSEHOLD EXPENSES DOCUMENT CHECKLIST

Include a copy or originals of the following documents with your _Life Management Portfolio: A How-To-Guide for Organizing Your Life._

Home Expenses Billing:

☐ Recent billing statement for all vendors

☐ Autopay bills have been identified and details provided

☐ Streaming services billing details provided

Notes - Explanation for items left unchecked:

_____
_____
_____
_____
_____
_____
_____
_____
_____

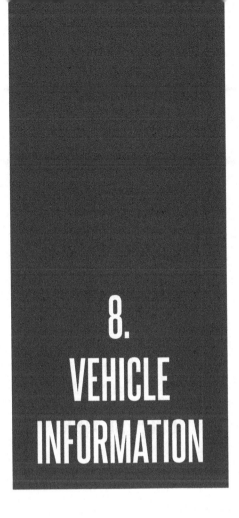

8.
VEHICLE INFORMATION

Most of us know to keep a vehicle's registration and insurance card in the glove box – but could you point to the location of your vehicle's title, latest financial statements or warranty if someone asked for it right now? We all agree that keeping some documents in the glove box is an easy way to organize and secure them in one location. *The Life Management Portfolio: A How-To-Guide for Organizing Your Life* aims to do that for all your documents and information—because even if a police officer pulling you over won't ever ask for them, anyone who needs to step into your shoes certainly might.

➢ *In this section, you will gather information regarding the following areas:*

VEHICLES – Whether you own or lease, it's imperative that you document details for all vehicles, and are in possession of each title, even those with lien holders. Vehicles can include cars, boats, motorcycles, All Terrain Vehicles (ATV's), trucks, and all other modes of transportation owned, leased or gifted.

FINANCE – Details on who you finance your vehicles with can help family members keep up with payments or make attempts to amend agreements depending on the circumstances they find themselves in. It can also help in facilitating sales or transfer of vehicle ownership, if needed.

VEHICLE INSURANCE – Vehicle insurance is a must! Just like your home, your vehicle is an asset you would want to protect.

EMERGENCY ROADSIDE ASSISTANCE – Your family may have different roadside assistance services for different vehicles, depending on your needs. Record the details here so you can easily manage accounts and information should changes be required.

HELPFUL TIPS

#1 Locate and secure titles to all vehicles.

#2 Be aware of leasing terms and conditions if the owner of said vehicle is unable to continue payments or passes away.

#3 Gifting a vehicle without changing ownership means you still own the vehicle.

VEHICLE INFORMATION

VEHICLES

VEHICLES	VEHICLE #1	VEHICLE #2
Make		
Model		
Year		
Color		
VIN #		
License Plate #		
Type of Vehicle		
Owned By (*name*)		
Registered To		
State Vehicle Registered In		
Vehicle Paid-In-Full	Yes / No	Yes / No
(*If yes*) Date Paid-In-Full		
Are you in possession of the title?	Yes / No (*If no, get it!*)	Yes / No (*If no, get it!*)
Dealership Name		
Dealership Phone #		
Salesperson's Name		
Salesperson's Cell Phone #		
Dealership Address		
Dealership City, State, Zip Code		
Is the vehicle leased?	Yes / No	Yes / No
(*If yes*) Leasing Company Name		
Leasing Company Phone #		
Vehicle Owner's Phone #		
Vehicle Owner's Cell Phone #		
Owner's Address		
City		
State		
Zip Code		

Additional Information & Updates: (Please be as specific as possible and date all changes.)

_____

_____

_____

_____
_____
_____
_____
_____
_____
_____

VEHICLES	VEHICLE #3	VEHICLE #4
Make		
Model		
Year		
Color		
VIN #		
License Plate #		
Type of Vehicle		
Owned By (_name_)		
Registered To		
State Vehicle Registered In		
Vehicle Paid-In-Full	Yes / No	Yes / No
(_If yes_) Date Paid-In-Full		
Are you in possession of the title?	Yes / No (_If no, get it!_)	Yes / No (_If no, get it!_)
Dealership Name		
Dealership Phone #		
Salesperson's Name		
Salesperson's Cell Phone #		
Dealership Address		
Dealership City, State, Zip Code		
Is the vehicle leased?	Yes / No	Yes / No
(_If yes_) Leasing Company Name		
Leasing Company Phone #		
Vehicle Owner's Phone #		
Vehicle Owner's Cell Phone #		
Owner's Address		
City		
State		
Zip Code		

Additional Information & Updates: (Please be as specific as possible and date all changes.)

_____
_____
_____
_____
_____
_____
_____
_____
_____
_____

FINANCE

FINANCE	VEHICLE #1	VEHICLE #2
Bank Name		
Bank Phone #		
Term of Loan		
Monthly Payment Amount	$	$
Billing Statement Received	Online / By Mail	Online / By Mail
Payments Made	Online / By Mail / Autopay / In-Person	Online / By Mail / Autopay / In-Person
How Often Payments Made	Mthly / Bi-Annually / Yearly	Mthly / Bi-Annually / Yearly
Vehicle Purchase Date		
Is the Vehicle Leased?	Yes / No	Yes / No
(If yes) Leasing Company Name		
Leasing Company Phone #		
Lease Expiration Date		
Loan Account #		
Account Holder's Name		
Account Holder's Phone #		
Account Holder's Cell Phone #		
Account Holder's Email Address		
Bank Website		
User Login		
User Password		
Pin #		
Security Word/Code		

Bank Address		
City		
State		
Zip Code		

Additional Information & Updates: (Please be as specific as possible and date all changes.)

_____
_____
_____
_____
_____
_____
_____
_____
_____
_____

FINANCE	VEHICLE #3	VEHICLE #4
Bank Name		
Bank Phone #		
Term of Loan		
Monthly Payment Amount	$	$
Billing Statement Received	Online / By Mail	Online / By Mail
Payments Made	Online / By Mail / Autopay / In-Person	Online / By Mail / Autopay / In-Person
How Often Payments Made	Mthly / Bi-Annually / Yearly	Mthly / Bi-Annually / Yearly
Vehicle Purchase Date		
Is the Vehicle Leased?	Yes / No	Yes / No
(If yes) Leasing Company Name		
Leasing Company Phone #		
Lease Expiration Date		
Loan Account #		
Account Holder's Name		
Account Holder's Phone #		
Account Holder's Cell Phone #		
Account Holder's Email Address		
Bank Website		
User Login		

User Password		
Pin #		
Security Word/Code		
Bank Address		
City		
State		
Zip Code		

Additional Information & Updates: (Please be as specific as possible and date all changes.)

_____

_____

_____

_____

_____

_____

_____

_____

_____

_____

_____

VEHICLE INSURANCE

VEHICLE INSURANCE	VEHICLE #1	VEHICLE #2
Insurance Company Name		
Company Phone #		
Agent Name		
Agent Cell Phone #		
Payment Amount	$	$
Billing Statement Received	Online / Mail	Online / Mail
Payments made	Online / By Mail / Autopay / In-Person	Online / By Mail / Autopay / In-Person
How Often Payments Made	Mthly / Bi-Annually / Yearly	Mthly / Bi-Annually / Yearly
Policy #		
Insured Policyholder Name		
Insured Policyholder Phone #		
Insured Policyholder Cell Phone #		
Insured Policyholder Email Address		

Insurance Company Website		
User Login		
User Password		
Pin #		
Security Word/Code		
Insurance Company Address		
City		
State		
Zip Code		

Additional Information & Updates: (Please be as specific as possible and date all changes.)

_____

_____

_____

_____

_____

_____

_____

_____

_____

_____

VEHICLE INSURANCE	VEHICLE #3	VEHICLE #4
Insurance Company Name		
Company Phone #		
Agent Name		
Agent Cell Phone #		
Payment Amount	$	$
Billing Statement Received	Online / Mail	Online / Mail
Payments made	Online / By Mail / Autopay / In-Person	Online / By Mail / Autopay / In-Person
How Often Payments Made	Mthly / Bi-Annually / Yearly	Mthly / Bi-Annually / Yearly
Policy #		
Insured Policyholder Name		
Insured Policyholder Phone #		
Insured Policyholder Cell Phone #		
Insured Policyholder Email Address		

Insurance Company Website		
User Login		
User Password		
Pin #		
Security Word/Code		
Insurance Company Address		
City		
State		
Zip Code		

Additional Information & Updates: (Please be as specific as possible and date all changes.)

_____
_____
_____
_____
_____
_____
_____
_____
_____
_____

EMERGENCY ROADSIDE ASSISTANCE

Provide details in the table below for each vehicle enrolled in an emergency roadside assistance service.

EMERGENCY ROADSIDE ASSISTANCE	VEHICLE #1	VEHICLE #2
Company Name		
Company Phone #		
Emergency Hotline #		
Coverage Start Date		
Expiration or Renewal Date		
Policy #		
Amount Paid	$	$
Billing Statement Received	Online / By Mail	Online / By Mail
Payments made?	Online / By Mail / Autopay / In-Person	Online / By Mail / Autopay / In-Person

How Often Payments Made	Mthly / Bi-Annually / Yearly	Mthly / Bi-Annually / Yearly
Policyholder Name		
Policyholder Phone #		
Policyholder Cell Phone #		
Policyholder Email Address		
Joint Policyholder Name		
Joint Policyholder Phone #		
Joint Policyholder Cell Phone #		
Company Website		
User Login		
User Password		
Pin #		
Security Word/Code		
Company Address		
City		
State		
Zip Code		

Additional Information & Updates: (Please be as specific as possible and date all changes.)

_____

_____

_____

_____

_____

_____

_____

_____

_____

_____

EMERGENCY ROADSIDE ASSISTANCE	VEHICLE #3	VEHICLE #4
Company Name		
Company Phone #		
Emergency Hotline #		
Coverage Start Date		
Expiration or Renewal Date		
Policy #		
Amount Paid	$	$

Billing Statement Received	Online / By Mail	Online / By Mail
Payments made?	Online / By Mail / Autopay / In-Person	Online / By Mail / Autopay / In-Person
How Often Payments Made	Mthly / Bi-Annually / Yearly	Mthly / Bi-Annually / Yearly
Policyholder Name		
Policyholder Phone #		
Policyholder Cell Phone #		
Policyholder Email Address		
Joint Policyholder Name		
Joint Policyholder Phone #		
Joint Policyholder Cell Phone #		
Company Website		
User Login		
User Password		
Pin #		
Security Word/Code		
Company Address		
City		
State		
Zip Code		

Additional Information & Updates: (Please be as specific as possible and date all changes.)

_____

_____

_____

_____

_____

_____

_____

_____

_____

VEHICLE INFORMATION DOCUMENT CHECKLIST

Include a copy or originals of the following documents with your *Life Management Portfolio: A How-To-Guide for Organizing Your Life.*

Vehicles:

☐ Vehicle titles *(even those with current liens)*

☐ Registration cards

☐ Insurance cards

☐ Vehicle warranty agreements (bumper-to-bumper, tires, computers, windshields, etc.)

☐ Vehicle maintenance & service records

Finance:

☐ Recent finance statement

Emergency Roadside Assistance:

☐ Roadside Assistance Identification Cards *(front and back)*

Notes - Explanation for items left unchecked:

_____

_____

_____

_____

_____

_____

_____

_____

_____

9.
LEGAL PROFILE

You or your family may have hired a lawyer to help with estate planning, lawsuits, advance directives, trusts, guardianship, or an array of other legal matters. Lawyers, by profession, also assist people in some of life's most high-stake matters, making it extremely important that you keep good records of your legal involvements and contacts in the event anyone needs to step in to help.

➤ *In this section, you will gather information regarding the following areas:*

LEGAL CASES – Not all legal cases concern an accusation of wrongdoing. Execution of wills, child support, alimony, divorce, accidents, real estate sales, and many regular matters of life may require a legal process and involve a lawyer. Give information on all cases and any lawyers or legal agencies you have worked with in the past.

HELPFUL TIPS

#1 Some lawyers specialize in long-term care, special needs and estate planning.

#2 You do not need to have a large estate to see value in estate planning.

#3 Estate planning involves, but is not limited to, making a will, setting up trusts, naming an executor (a person responsible for overseeing and managing how assets will be handled), and beneficiaries, to name a few.

#4 Assets include, but not limited to, houses, land, cars and financial accounts.

LEGAL PROFILE

LEGAL CASE #1	
Name of Family Member Involved	
Docket #/Case Name	
Current Case Status	Active / Resolved
Other Parties Involved	
Short Description of Issue Under Dispute	
Firm Name	
Lawyer Name	
Lawyer Office Phone #	
Lawyer Cell Phone #	
Lawyer Email	
Lawyer Fax #	
Law Firm Address	
City	
State	
Zip Code	

Additional Information & Updates: (Please be as specific as possible and date all changes.)

_____

_____

_____

_____

_____

_____

_____

_____

_____

_____

LEGAL CASE #2	
Name of Family Member Involved	
Docket #/Case Name	

Current Case Status	Active / Resolved
Other Parties Involved	
Short Description of Issue Under Dispute	
Firm Name	
Lawyer Name	
Lawyer Office Phone #	
Lawyer Cell Phone #	
Lawyer Email	
Lawyer Fax #	
Law Firm Address	
City	
State	
Zip Code	

Additional Information & Updates: (Please be as specific as possible and date all changes.)

_____
_____
_____
_____
_____
_____
_____
_____
_____
_____

LEGAL CASE #3	
Name of Family Member Involved	
Docket #/Case Name	
Current Case Status	Active / Resolved
Other Parties Involved	
Short Description of Issue Under Dispute	

Firm Name	
Lawyer Name	
Lawyer Office Phone #	
Lawyer Cell Phone #	
Lawyer Email	
Lawyer Fax #	
Law Firm Address	
City	
State	
Zip Code	

Additional Information & Updates: (Please be as specific as possible and date all changes.)

_____

_____

_____

_____

_____

_____

_____

_____

_____

LEGAL PROFILE DOCUMENT CHECKLIST

Include a copy or originals of the following documents with your *Life Management Portfolio: A How-To-Guide for Organizing Your Life.*

Legal Profile:

☐ Estate Planning Legal Documentation

☐ Pre/Post Nuptial Agreements

☐ Separation Arrangements

☐ Spousal Support Agreements

☐ Child Support Agreements

☐ Wage Garnishment Details

☐ Accident lawsuits – include supportive medical documentation

☐ Other:

Notes - Explanation for items left unchecked:

_____
_____
_____
_____
_____
_____
_____
_____
_____

10.
ADVANCE
DIRECTIVES

Advance directives are legal documents expressing a person's direct wishes for their care, should they become unable to make or express decisions for themselves. They specifically outline your medical care preferences, instead of leaving decisions to loved ones who may have differences of opinions amongst themselves. Each directive should have a designated and an alternative agent who will be responsible for ensuring that the patient's care abides by the wishes stipulated in each directive.

Putting advance directives in place and working through this portion of your Portfolio may be an emotional process. The purpose of these documents, and the conversations they will lead you to have with your loved ones, is to give you the comfort of knowing that your life will ultimately continue in the manner of your own choosing, and that your family will not have to bear the weight of those difficult decisions.

➢ *In this section, you will gather information regarding the following areas:*

LIVING WILL — A living will documents your instructions for end-of-life medical treatment(s) you do and do not want, such as artificial hydration (IV, or intravenous fluids), artificial nutrition (feeding tubes), and mechanical ventilation in the event you are unable to communicate. Consult with an attorney or health care professional, as laws in each state vary. A will is different from a living will, as a will becomes effective upon death.

DURABLE HEALTH CARE POWER OF ATTORNEY/HEALTH CARE PROXY — In the event you are unconscious or unable to make or communicate decisions for yourself, a Durable Health Care Power of Attorney/Health Care Proxy will enable an agent (also known as a health care proxy) to make informed medical care decisions on your behalf.

DURABLE POWER OF ATTORNEY FOR FINANCES — There can be many layers involved in the execution of this advanced directive, therefore it is advisable to consult with a legal professional in deciding what would be best for you. While a Durable Power of Attorney for Finances will allow a person (agent or attorney-in-fact) to handle legal, business and financial affairs on your behalf, note the difference between general power, limited power and durable power of attorney. General power of attorney applies to a multitude of various transactions, while limited power of attorney may be more targeted to a specific situation. Durable Power of Attorney remains in effect in cases of mental incapacity, as opposed to a general power of attorney that becomes null when a person is deemed mentally incapable of making decisions. Designate an agent that you trust! An agent will have the power to withdraw money from your accounts, sell and purchase homes in your name, and open and close accounts on your behalf. This sort of financial power comes with the potential for abuse and fraudulent behavior, so be mindful to seek professional or legal advice prior to implementing this advance directive.

MEDICAL ORDERS — Advanced medical orders express a patient's medical preference in the form of a doctor's order. Examples may include Do Not Resuscitate Order (DNR), Do Not Intubate Order (DNI), Medical Orders for Life-Sustaining Treatment (MOLST), and Physician Orders for Life-Sustaining Treatment (POLST). Check with your health care provider for the appropriate forms used in your state.

For more in-depth information on advance directives or medical orders, please consult with a social worker, lawyer or your health care provider.

HELPFUL TIPS

#1 Every state has different advance directive forms. Make sure you're using the correct forms for your state if you're going to complete your own forms.

#2 Keep your advance directives up-to-date. You should review all legal documents at least every six months. Should your agents become unavailable due to their own sickness, death, or a change in your relationship with that person, a bi-annual review will allow you an opportunity to make any necessary adjustments.

#3 Provide copies of your advance directives to your physicians and designated agents.

#4 A Durable Power of Attorney for Finances becomes invalid once a person dies. Once a person is deceased, the responsibility of the agent can no longer continue unless he or she is also listed as an executor in a will or appointed by the courts as an administrator of the deceased estate (if a will has not been executed).

#5 Eighteen-year-olds are legal adults and therefore responsible for their own health care decisions by law. Educate your young adult on the necessity of executing an advance directive. Who would they want to make health care decisions for them, if needed?

#6 Some legal departments on college campuses offer assistance with executing advance directives for free.

#7 Some law firms provide free educational seminars on advance directives.

10. ADVANCE DIRECTIVES

LIVING WILL

(If you have included an original Living Will with your portfolio, you may skip this section.)

LIVING WILL	FAMILY MEMBER #1	FAMILY MEMBER #2
Family Member Name		
Do you have a living will?	Yes / No	Yes / No
(If yes) Do you have an updated copy?	Yes / No	Yes / No
(If yes) Date Last Updated		
Is your document notarized?	Yes / No (*If no, it's invalid*)	Yes / No (*If no, it's invalid*)
Who drafted the document?	Self / Other	Self / Other
If Other: State the person's name		
Other: Office Phone #		
Other: Cell Phone #		
Other: Email Address		
Other: Address		
Other: City		
Other: State		
Other: Zip Code		
Is your designated agent alive?	Yes / No	Yes / No
Do you need to change agents?	Yes / No (*If yes, do so ASAP*)	Yes / No (*If yes, do so ASAP*)
Designated Agent Name		
Designated Agent Phone #		
Designated Agent Cell Phone #		
Designated Agent Email Address		
Designated Agent Address		
City		
State		
Zip Code		
Is there an alternate agent?	Yes / No	Yes / No
Is the alternate agent alive?	Yes / No	Yes / No
Do you need to change agents?	Yes / No (*If yes, do so ASAP*)	Yes / No (*If yes, do so ASAP*)
Alternate Agent Name		
Alternate Agent Phone #		

Alternate Agent Cell Phone #		
Alternate Agent Email Address		
Alternate Agent Address		
City		
State		
Zip Code		

Additional Information & Updates: (Please be as specific as possible and date all changes.)

_____

_____

_____

_____

_____

_____

_____

_____

_____

_____

DURABLE HEALTH CARE POWER OF ATTORNEY/HEALTH CARE PROXY

(If you have included an original Durable Health Care Power of Attorney/Health Care Proxy with your portfolio, you may skip this section.)

DURABLE POWER OF ATTORNEY FOR HEALTH CARE	FAMILY MEMBER #1	FAMILY MEMBER #2
Family Member Name		
Do you have a health care proxy?	Yes / No	Yes / No
(If yes) Do you have an updated copy?	Yes / No	Yes / No
(If yes) Date Last Updated		
Is your document notarized?	Yes / No (If no, it's invalid)	Yes / No (If no, it's invalid)
Who drafted the document?	Self / Other:	Self / Other:
If Other: state the person's name		
Other: Office Phone #		
Other: Cell Phone #		
Other: Email Address		
Other: Address		

Other: City		
Other: State		
Other: Zip Code		
Is Your Agent Alive	Yes / No	Yes / No
Do you need to change agents?	Yes / No (*If yes, do so ASAP*)	Yes / No (*If yes, do so ASAP*)
Designated Agent Name		
Designated Agent Phone #		
Designated Agent Cell Phone #		
Designated Agent Email Address		
Designated Agent Address		
City		
State		
Zip Code		
Is there an alternate agent?	Yes / No	Yes / No
Is the alternate agent alive?	Yes / No	Yes / No
Do you need to change agents?	Yes / No (*If yes, do so ASAP*)	Yes / No (*If yes, do so ASAP*)
Alternate Agent Name		
Alternate Agent Phone #		
Alternate Agent Cell Phone #		
Alternate Agent Email Address		
Alternate Agent Address		
City		
State		
Zip Code		

Additional Information & Updates: (Please be as specific as possible and date all changes.)

_____

_____

_____

_____

_____

_____

_____

_____

_____

DURABLE POWER OF ATTORNEY FOR FINANCES

(If you have included an original Durable Power of Attorney for Finances with your portfolio, you may skip this section.)

DURABLE POWER OF ATTORNEY FOR FINANCES	FAMILY MEMBER #1	FAMILY MEMBER #2
Family Member Name		
Do you have a power of attorney?	Yes / No	Yes / No
(If yes) Do you have an updated copy?	Yes / No	Yes / No
(If yes) Date Last Updated		
Is your document notarized?	Yes / No (If no, it's invalid)	Yes / No (If no, it's invalid)
Who drafted the document?	Self / Other:	Self / Other:
If Other: State the person's name		
Other: Office Phone #		
Other: Cell Phone #		
Other: Email Address		
Other: Address		
Other: City		
Other: State		
Other: Zip Code		
Is Your Agent Alive	Yes / No	Yes / No
Do you need to change agents?	Yes / No (If yes, do so ASAP)	Yes / No (If yes, do so ASAP)
Designated Agent Name		
Designated Agent Phone #		
Designated Agent Cell Phone #		
Designated Agent Email Address		
Designated Agent Address		
City		
State		
Zip Code		
Is there an alternate agent?	Yes / No	Yes / No
Is the alternate agent alive?	Yes / No	Yes / No
Do you need to change agents?	Yes / No (If yes, do so ASAP)	Yes / No (If yes, do so ASAP)
Alternate Agent Name		
Alternate Agent Phone #		
Alternate Agent Cell Phone #		
Alternate Agent Email Address		
Alternate Agent Address		
City		

State		
Zip Code		

Additional Information & Updates: (Please be as specific as possible and date all changes.)

_____

_____

_____

_____

_____

_____

_____

_____

_____

10.1 MEDICAL ORDERS

DO NOT RESUSCITATE (DNR)

A DNR is a doctor's written order that instructs healthcare workers to refrain from performing cardiopulmonary resuscitation (CPR) if a person stops breathing or if their heart stops beating. *(If you have included an original Do Not Resuscitate order with your portfolio, you may skip this section.)*

DO NOT RESUSCITATE (DNR)	FAMILY MEMBER #1	FAMILY MEMBER #2
Family Member Name		
Do you have a DNR?	Yes / No	Yes / No
(If yes) Do you have an updated copy?	Yes / No	Yes / No
(If yes) Date Last Updated		
Is the DNR signed by a doctor?	Yes / No *(If no, it's invalid)*	Yes / No *(If no, it's invalid)*
Doctor who ordered the DNR		
Doctor's Office Phone #		
Doctor's Cell Phone #		
Doctor's Email Address		
Doctor's Office Address		
City		
State		
Zip Code		

Additional Information & Updates: (Please be as specific as possible and date all changes.)

_____
_____
_____
_____
_____
_____
_____
_____
_____
_____

DO NOT INTUBATE (DNI)

Chest compressions and cardiac drugs may be used during care, but breathing tubes will not be inserted into a patient. *(If you have included an original Do Not Intubate order with your portfolio, you may skip this section.)*

DO NOT INTUBATE (DNI)	FAMILY MEMBER #1	FAMILY MEMBER #2
Family Member Name		
Do you have a DNI?	Yes / No	Yes / No
(If yes) Do you have an updated copy?	Yes / No	Yes / No
(If yes) Date Last Updated		
Is the DNI signed by a doctor?	Yes / No *(If no, it's invalid)*	Yes / No *(If no, it's invalid)*
Doctor who ordered the DNI		
Doctor's Office Phone #		
Doctor's Cell Phone #		
Doctor's Email Address		
Doctor's Office Address		
City		
State		
Zip Code		

Additional Information & Updates: (Please be as specific as possible and date all changes.)

_____
_____
_____
_____
_____
_____
_____
_____
_____

MEDICAL ORDERS FOR LIFE-SUSTAINING TREATMENT (MOLST)

Applicable in some states, the MOLST form is used to facilitate end-of-life medical decisions by documenting a patient's treatment preferences. *(If you have included original Medical Orders for Life-Sustaining Treatment with your portfolio, you may skip this section.)*

MEDICAL ORDERS FOR LIFE-SUSTAINING TREATMENT (MOLST)	FAMILY MEMBER #1	FAMILY MEMBER #2
Family Member Name		
Do you have a MOLST?	Yes / No	Yes / No
(If yes) Do you have an updated copy?	Yes / No	Yes / No
(If yes) Date Last Updated		
Is the MOLST signed by a doctor?	Yes / No (*If no, it's invalid*)	Yes / No (*If no, it's invalid*)
Doctor who ordered MOLST		
Doctor's Office Phone #		
Doctor's Cell Phone #		
Doctor's Email Address		
Doctor's Office Address		
City		
State		
Zip Code		

Additional Information & Updates: (Please be as specific as possible and date all changes.)

_____

_____

_____

_____

_____

_____

_____

_____

_____

_____

PHYSICIAN ORDERS FOR LIFE-SUSTAINING TREATMENT (POLST)

Applicable in some states, POLST is a care planning tool for seriously ill patients (living approximately one year or less) desiring more control over end-of-life care. *(If you have included original Physician Orders for Life-Sustaining Treatment with your portfolio, you may skip this section.)*

PHYSICIAN ORDERS FOR LIFE-SUSTAINING TREATMENT (POLST)	FAMILY MEMBER #1	FAMILY MEMBER #2
Family Member Name		
Do you have a POLST?	Yes / No	Yes / No
(If yes) Do you have an updated copy?	Yes / No	Yes / No
(If yes) Date Last Updated		
Is the POLST signed by a doctor?	Yes / No (If no, it's invalid)	Yes / No (If no, it's invalid)
Doctor who ordered POLST		
Doctor's Office Phone #		
Doctor's Cell Phone #		
Doctor's Email Address		
Doctor's Office Address		
City		
State		
Zip Code		

Additional Information & Updates: (Please be as specific as possible and date all changes.)

_____
_____
_____
_____
_____
_____
_____
_____
_____
_____

ORGAN DONATION

ORGAN DONATION	FAMILY MEMBER #1	FAMILY MEMBER #2
Family Member Name		
Organ Donor	Yes / No	Yes / No
(If yes) Do you have an organ donor card?	Yes / No	Yes / No

Donor Card Identification #		
Listed as a donor on Driver's License	Yes / No	Yes / No
Specify body part for donation *(Check all that apply)*	All Organs / Eyes / Tissue Donor	All Organs / Eyes / Tissue Donor
	☐ Corneas Only	☐ Corneas Only
	☐ Face Only	☐ Face Only
	☐ Hands Only	☐ Hands Only
	☐ Heart Only	☐ Heart Only
	☐ Intestines Only	☐ Intestines Only
	☐ Kidneys Only	☐ Kidneys Only
	☐ Liver Only	☐ Liver Only
	☐ Lungs Only	☐ Lungs Only
	☐ Pancreas Only	☐ Pancreas Only
	☐ Tissue Only	☐ Tissue Only

Additional Information & Updates: (Please be as specific as possible and date all changes.)

_____

_____

_____

_____

_____

_____

_____

_____

_____

_____

ADVANCE DIRECTIVES DOCUMENT CHECKLIST

Include a copy or originals of the following documents with your *Life Management Portfolio: A-How-To-Guide for Organizing Your Life.*

Advance Directives:

☐ Living Will/Will

☐ Durable Power of Attorney for Health Care

☐ Durable Power of Attorney for Finances

☐ Do Not Resuscitate Order (DNR)

☐ Do Not Intubate Order (DNI)

☐ MOLST Form

☐ POLST Form

☐ Organ Donor Card and/or Driver's License proving organ donation *(front and back)*

☐ College Student 18 years-of-age and older Durable Power of Attorney for Health Care Form

☐ Speak to a health care professional about advance directives and Medical Orders

Notes - Explanation for items left unchecked:

_____

_____

_____

_____

_____

_____

_____

_____

_____

_____

11.
FINAL WISHES

As you reach this final section, know that you have done so much already to prepare yourself and your family for life's unexpected events. You've probably had a few sit-downs with your loved ones and discussed a few difficult matters, and I encourage you to hold each other with the same closeness as you face this ultimate topic: death.

Death is part of life, and as much as we'd like to believe it will never happen, it's the one thing we know to be inevitable. In the face of that certainty, let your *Life Management Portfolio: A How-To-Guide for Organizing Your Life* prepare you and your family to face that eventuality with as much grace as possible. As you reflect, plan, and set decisions down in this workbook, as difficult as they may be, know that these directions will offer your family a measure of peace someday in the future.

 In this section, you will gather information regarding the following areas:

FUNERAL HOME – With all the options out there, give some thought on which company you believe would best serve your needs with grace, dignity and respect.

BURIAL – A burial involves many details and decisions. Don't leave your family to guess at what would be best; take time in thinking about it now and make your wishes known.

CREMATION – People tend to have strong feelings about this option. Just like with burial, the only way for your family to know your preferences is by telling them.

FUNERAL SERVICE – Funeral services can vary greatly depending on religion, personal wishes, family traditions, or other characteristics of a person. What's your style?

SPECIAL REQUESTS – This is a chance to reflect who you are and what you want. Special requests can be anything: songs, pallbearers, poems, a color for guest attire. What's most important to you?

HELPFUL TIPS

#1 Don't overthink. This section is about being prepared and proactive, and nothing more.

#2 For veterans who may be eligible for Veterans Administration (VA) burial benefits and memorial items, visit www.va.gov.

#3 Life insurance policies are crucial to ensuring your family's continued care and well-being after death.

#4 Funeral Directors should also be presented with life insurance information to assist a family in using its benefits.

#5 Policies must be up-to-date with beneficiaries who are alive and still in your life.

#6 Pre-burial accounts should be verified periodically.

#7 Writing can be a slower and more honest form of communication. If you're not comfortable talking about this topic, write it down.

#8 Many times, family members either struggle to fill in the blanks of an obituary or only learn some fascinating detail about a person after their death. Write a story about your life and leave it with this workbook—or better yet, share it with your family now.

#9 Based on an AARP survey conducted in 2017, 60% of Americans do not have a will or have not engaged in any estate planning. If that includes you, start the process of executing a will today.

FINAL WISHES

FUNERAL HOME

FUNERAL HOME	FAMILY MEMBER #1	FAMILY MEMBER #2
Family Member Name		
Funeral Home Name		
Office Phone #		
Person of Contact Name		
Person of Contact Cell Phone #		
Pre-Arranged Funeral Plan	Yes / No	Yes / No
(If yes) Account/Policy #		
Pre-Burial Plan	Yes / No	Yes / No
(If yes) Account/Policy #		
Funeral Home Website		
Address		
City		
State		
Zip Code		

Additional Information & Updates: (Please be as specific as possible and date all changes.)

_____
_____
_____
_____
_____
_____
_____
_____
_____

BURIAL

BURIAL	FAMILY MEMBER #1	FAMILY MEMBER #2
Family Member Name		
Name of Cemetery		

Cemetery Phone #		
Person of Contact Name		
Person of Contact Cell Phone #		
Plot Account/ID #		
Plot Section/Row/Space #		
Is the plot a shared space?	Yes / No	Yes / No
Tombstone/Headstone	Yes / No	Yes / No
Grave Marker	Yes / No	Yes / No
Cemetery Website		
Address		
City		
State		
Zip Code		

Additional Information & Updates: (Please be as specific as possible and date all changes.)

_____
_____
_____
_____
_____
_____
_____
_____
_____
_____
_____

CREMATION

CREMATION	FAMILY MEMBER #1	FAMILY MEMBER #2
Family Member Name		
Do you wish to be cremated?	Yes / No	Yes / No
(If yes) **Crematory Name**		
Crematory Phone #		
Person of Contact Name		
Person of Contact Cell Phone #		
Pre-Arranged Cremation Service	Yes / No	Yes / No

(If yes) Account/Policy #		
Type of Urn		
Crematory Website		
Address		
City		
State		
Zip Code		

Additional Information & Updates: (Please be as specific as possible and date all changes.)

_____

_____

_____

_____

_____

_____

_____

_____

_____

_____

FUNERAL SERVICE

FUNERAL SERVICE	FAMILY MEMBER #1	FAMILY MEMBER #2
Family Member Name		
Place of Worship Name		
Place of Worship Phone #		
Person of Contact Name		
Clergy/Pastor/Rabbi/Other		
Are You a Member?	Yes / No	Yes / No
Place of Worship Service Fee	$	$
Place of Worship Website		
Address		
City		
State		
Zip Code		

Additional Information & Updates: (Please be as specific as possible and date all changes.)

_____

_____

_____

_____

_____

_____

_____

_____

_____

SPECIAL REQUESTS

SPECIAL REQUESTS	FAMILY MEMBER #1	FAMILY MEMBER #2
Family Member Name		
Clothing Color		
Casket/Urn Color		
Special Request Regarding Ashes		
Florist Name		
Florist Phone #		
Florist Address/City/State		
Soloists Name		
Soloists Cell Phone #		
Organist Name		
Organist Cell Phone #		
Song Selection #1		
Song Selection #2		
Old Testament Scripture Verse		
New Testament Scripture Verse		
Obituary Designer's Name		
Obituary Designer Cell Phone #		
Obituary Details	Attach – Brag About Yourself!	Attach – Brag About Yourself!
Open Casket for Viewing?	Yes / No	Yes / No
Pallbearer's Name #1		

Pallbearer's Name #2		
Pallbearer's Name #3		
Pallbearer's Name #4		
Pallbearer's Name #5		
Pallbearer's Name #6		
Other:		
Other:		

Additional Information & Updates: (Please be as specific as possible and date all changes.)

_____

_____

_____

_____

_____

_____

_____

_____

_____

FINAL WISHES DOCUMENT CHECKLIST

Include a copy or originals of the following documents with your *Life Management Portfolio: A How-To-Guide for Organizing Your Life.*

Final Wishes:

☐ Last Will and Testament

☐ Pre-Arranged Funeral Plan

☐ Pre-Arranged Burial Plan

☐ Pre-Arranged Cremation Plan

☐ Life Insurance Policy

☐ Veterans Administration (VA) Sponsored Life Insurance Policy

☐ Obituary details – Write your life story!

Notes - Explanation for items left unchecked:

_____

_____

_____

_____

_____

_____

_____

_____

_____

_____

12.
CHARITABLE
DONATIONS

C ontinue your philanthropic efforts by documenting your history of giving and your wishes in this section. Send a positive message to those who may oversee your affairs: It's always better to give than to receive!

CHARITABLE DONATIONS

CHARITABLE DONATIONS	ORGANIZATION #1	ORGANIZATION #2
Organization Name		
Company Phone #		
Contact Representative		
Charity Mission/Cause		
Donated Amount	$	$
Donation Made	Mthly / Bi-Annually / Yearly	Mthly / Bi-Annually / Yearly
Organization's Website		
Organization's Address		

City		
State		
Zip Code		

CHARITABLE DONATIONS	ORGANIZATION #3	ORGANIZATION #4
Organization Name		
Company Phone #		
Contact Representative		
Charity Mission/Cause		
Donated Amount	$	$
Donation Made	Mthly / Bi-Annually / Yearly	Mthly / Bi-Annually / Yearly
Organization's Website		
Organization's Address		
City		
State		
Zip Code		

Additional Information & Updates: (Please be as specific as possible and date all changes.)

_____

_____

_____

_____

_____

_____

_____

_____

CHARITABLE DONATIONS DOCUMENT CHECKLIST

Include a copy or originals of the following documents with your *Life Management Portfolio: A How-To-Guide for Organizing Your Life.*

Charitable Donations:

☐ Donation Receipts

☐ Records of Tax Deductions on Charitable Donations

☐ Organizational Agreements

Notes - Explanation for items left unchecked:

_____
_____
_____
_____
_____
_____
_____
_____
_____
_____

13.
ONLINE ACCOUNTS & LOGIN CREDENTIALS

How often have you forgotten the username or password to one of your many online accounts? Completing this chart will keep you from having to click that pesky "Forgot Your Password" button and help you (or anyone acting on your behalf) access your information more quickly and seamlessly.

HELPFUL TIPS

#1 Update your passwords at least once every six months. Use symbols and special characters (such as #, @, or $) to strengthen your passwords.

#2 Companies will not contact you to verify passwords or account information.

#3 Do not click on or open suspicious emails.

#4 Beware of technical support attempts to gain access to your computer. Verify details with your tech support or warranty company.

#5 Enable 2-Step Verification whenever possible to fend off fraudulent attempts to access your accounts.

DEVICE CREDENTIALS

(May include laptops, tablets, smartwatches).

DEVICE	PASSWORD/PASSCODE

ONLINE ACCOUNTS & LOGIN CREDENTIALS

WEBSITE	USERNAME	PASSWORD	UPDATED PASSWORD

Additional Information & Updates: (Please be as specific as possible and date all changes.)

_____

_____

_____

_____

_____

_____

_____

_____

_____

_____

ANNUAL REVIEW FORM

It is imperative that the information in *The Life Management Portfolio: A How-To-Guide for Organizing Your Life* stays up-to-date. In addition to updating your information as important life changes occur, it's highly recommended that you review all sections in your profile on an annual basis.

Please date and sign below to indicate that an annual review has been completed.

YEAR	DATE OF REVIEW	SIGNATURE

DISASTER PREPAREDNESS GUIDE

Natural disasters have become increasingly frequent and violent over the years. With hurricanes, tornadoes, floods and alarming shifts in weather patterns regularly making the news, the need for preparation is crucial. Take the necessary precautions and action steps *before* a natural disaster or emergency strikes.

Be aware of the critical steps to safeguarding your home and identify the essentials needed to keep you and your family safe. The following tips and checklist will help you make a response plan for any event that may call upon you to evacuate your home, or to shelter in place for an extended period of time.

For a more comprehensive guide to preparing for a natural disaster, visit www.ready. gov.

FAMILY DISASTER PREPAREDNESS CHECKLIST:

- ☐ Locate and label emergency shut off valve for water, power, gas, and heating for all properties
- ☐ Family emergency evacuation plan
- ☐ Battery operated radio, flashlights and batteries
- ☐ Gallons of water for sanitation (flushing toilets, washing, etc.)
- ☐ Gallon of water per day/per household member for three days
- ☐ Three days' supply of non-perishable food (peanut butter, cereal, granola bars, canned meats, beans)
- ☐ Manual can opener
- ☐ Sleeping bags
- ☐ First aid kit (gloves, bandages, rubbing alcohol, peroxide, ibuprofen)
- ☐ Install weather alert notification on cell phone(s)

Pet Disaster Preparedness Checklist:

- ☐ Five day's supply of pet food and water
- ☐ Food/water bowls
- ☐ Leash/harness
- ☐ Paper towels
- ☐ Trash bags
- ☐ Pet wipes
- ☐ Extra blankets and bedding

- ☐ *Your Life Management Portfolio: A How-To-Guide for Organizing Your Life!*

Additional Items:

_____

_____

_____

_____

_____

_____

_____

_____

_____

CONCLUSION

Think back to the version of you who first picked up this book. If you were anything like the majority of people, you probably had some idea of the state of your financial accounts, where you kept your important documents, whether you had a life insurance plan...but you probably hadn't looked at that policy since the day it was purchased. You probably had your documents spread over several locations, locked in drawers or hidden under floorboards. And you likely had never told anyone, even your close family, how to access your household bills, or any other accounts, in the event that they needed to do so.

Now, take a look around. You have made it to the end of this workbook! You've tackled one of the most difficult tasks most people choose to avoid or ignore, and your family is stronger for it. In a world where accidents, illness, superstorms and even death are unavoidable realities, you and your family's preparedness is a testament to your love and your care for one another, and you should be proud.

Your completed *Life Management Portfolio: A How-To-Guide for Organizing Your Life* is now ready to spring into action for you the moment it's needed. Let it be your road-map through life's uncertain moments, big and small. Let it be a key for caretakers to unlock your world. And let it be an occasion to check in with your family, to reassure one another and to continue the practice of honest conversation that helps you weather any storm.

CONGRATULATIONS!

FINAL NOTE: It is highly advisable that you keep your *Life Management Portfolio: A How-To-Guide for Organizing Your Life* safe and secure at all times. There is a wealth of confidential personal information contained on each page of your portfolio. Do not leave it casually sitting around, on bookshelves, or in any open area where its contents can be viewed, copied, manipulated or stolen. It is advisable to store your *Life Management Portfolio: A How-To-Guide for Organizing Your Life* in a locked, waterproof and fireproof location. The same vigilance you take in keeping your social security, birth certificate and financial documents secure, you are advised to do the same with your Portfolio.

ACKNOWLEDGMENTS

This workbook is a true testament to God using my personal pain and professional experience to highlight an unspoken ordeal many families encounter during a crisis.

Thank you to my husband, children, parents, and best-friend for your love and support in manifesting my vision.

I want to thank my Editor, Tenyia Lee, for your unwavering support and collaboration in brilliantly fine-tuning ten years worth of research, thoughts and notes, and bringing them to life. I also want to thank Proofed and Perfected for the impeccable proofreading and line-editing service, and managing my perfectionism.

RESOURCES

Veterans Administration – www.va.gov

Social Security Administration – www.ssa.gov

Medicare – www.medicare.gov

Medicaid – www.medicaid.gov

Disability Services – www.usa.gov/disability-services

Alzheimer's Association – www.alz.org

American Stroke Association – www.stroke.org

Official Guide to Government Information and Services – www.usa.gov

American Red Cross – www.redcross.gov

Plan Ahead for Disasters – www.ready.gov

ABOUT THE AUTHOR

Anni B. Johnson is a Licensed Master Social Worker who has worked with families and individuals for nearly thirty years, helping them navigate the complexities of life.

Anni's life purpose of renewing, rebuilding and restoring relationships remains at the core of everything she does. As an author, speaker and relationship coach, she continues to write and educate communities and families about the importance of preparedness, relationship-building, and living life from the inside out.

For client inquiries, speaking engagements, or vendor opportunities, and to learn more about Anni and how God continues to use her to uplift, encourage and impact the lives of others, visit annibjohnson.com or follow her on all social media platforms @annibjohnson.

Made in the USA
Columbia, SC
17 October 2022